Madrid

COLLINS
Glasgow & London

Plaza Mayor

First published 1990
Copyright © William Collins Sons & Company Limited
Published by William Collins Sons & Company Limited
Printed in Hong Kong
ISBN 0 00 435779-5

HOW TO USE THIS BOOK

Your Collins Traveller Guide will help you find your way around your chosen destination quickly and easily. It is colour-coded for easy reference:

The blue-coded 'topic' section answers the question 'I would like to see or do something; where do I go and what do I see when I get there?' A simple, clear layout provides an alphabetical list of activities and events, offers you a selection of each, tells you how to get there, what it will cost, when it is open and what to expect. Each topic in the list has its own simplified map, showing the position of each item and the nearest landmark or transport access, for instant orientation. Whether your interest is Architecture or Sport you can find all the information you need quickly and simply. Where major resorts within an area require in-depth treatment, they follow the main topics section in alphabetical order.

The red-coded section is a lively and informative gazetteer. In one alphabetical list you can find essential facts about the main places and cultural items - 'What is La Bastille?', 'Who was Michelangelo?' - as well as practical and invaluable travel information. It covers everything you need to know to help you enjoy yourself and get the most out of your time away, from Accommodation through Babysitters, Car Hire, Food, Health, Money, Newspapers, Taxis and Telephones to Zoos.

Cross-references: Type in small capitals - **CHURCHES** - tells you that more information on an item is available within the topic on churches. A-Z in bold - **A-Z** - tells you that more information is available on an item within the gazetteer. Simply look under the appropriate heading. A name in bold - **Holy Cathedral** - also tells you that more information on an item is available in the gazetteer under that particular heading.

Packed full of information and easy to use - you'll always know where you are with your Collins Traveller Guide!

Puerto Del Sol

Photographs by **Jan Kruse**
Cover picture by **Travel Photo International**

Plaza de la Ville de Paris

When in 1561 Phillip II, then the world's most powerful ruler, moved his seat of government to Madrid, it was a small, dusty town beside the meagre Manzaneres river on the high plateau of Castile near Spain's geographical centre. Today, it is an expanding, modern city of five million people. Since Phillip's time, Madrid has been Spain's capital in every sense, holding the nation's pulse and pulling the strings. Even now, when some autonomy has been devolved to Spain's 17 regions, it is essentially in Madrid that high-fliers of Spanish politics, business and the arts must make their mark.

As Spain has returned to the world stage and its economy has boomed, Madrid is increasingly courted by foreign politicians and business people. For other visitors Madrid's rich art collections, like that of the renowned Prado, and its many interesting museums are the big attractions. Others find contemporary Madrid's main appeal within its creative ferment and frenetic lifestyle ushered in by the blooming of democracy since General Franco's death in 1975.

La Movida was the name given to Spain's cultural revival led by Madrid. Talented people, many young and uninhibited, used their new freedom to experiment creatively and follow fresh lifestyles. Local and national government began supporting the arts to an extent that most of the world's cities would envy. A drab dictatorship's stuffy capital was energized and became a bright star of the avant garde. Suddenly, Madrid was 'in'. And so it has remained.

Contemporary culture is on show in the many exhibition halls, art galleries, and bouyant cultural centres like the Centro Cultural de la Villa and Centro de Arte Reina Sofia. Classic and modern plays, both Spanish and foreign, are presented in some 30 theatres and fringe drama is growing. The world's top performers contribute to the opera, ballet and classical music seasons. Not that Spain is short of home-grown talents. The pop, rock and jazz scenes are lively and often feature big, open-air events. At last, Madrid is again the cultural capital of the Spanish-speaking world.

The new *Madrileños* are gregarious, fashion-mad and culture-hungry. Youth and beauty are social assets. Talent or wealth help. Captives of their city's whirling blithe spirit, they meet at smart bars, cafés and summertime *terrazas*, modern designer boutiques, at the openings of new

shows and exhibitions, and at clubs where they dance graceful sevillanas. And they get by with very little sleep. Their favourite discos don't get lively before three in the morning. It's tiring just watching them and utterly exhausting keeping pace.

Meal times too are late. Lunch starts after two and dinner around ten. But appetising *tapas* in hundreds of traditional *tascas* can keep hunger at bay. Or there are cafés, cafeterias and fast-food places. Eating well in Madrid's old *mesones* and many good restaurants is inexpensive compared with other European capitals. All the diverse cuisines of Spain's regions can be enjoyed. *Madrileños* demand the freshest of fish. Restaurants take care not to disappoint them.

The most likely budget wrecker during a stay in Madrid will be the lure of its shops. Madrid, like Barcelona, is a new hotspot in the world of fashion and design. Boutiques and shops offer the latest clothes, accessories and other creations of Spain's acclaimed new designers. Old-world shops sell their traditional, handmade products. Examples of Spain's best craftwork are available in many *artesanias*. Antiques can be another good buy. For an experience more than for serious buying, there's El Rastro, a large, bustling fleamarket.

Tourist Madrid is quite compact. Buses and the metro are easy to use. Taxis are plentiful and cheap. Old 'Hapsburg' Madrid centres on the Plaza Major, extending southwards into a maze of narrow streets, south east towards lively Plaza de Santa Ana and westwards to the huge, ornate Palacio Real. 'Bourbon' Madrid includes the Prado museum and the welcoming, always interesting, Retiro park. The wide, tree-lined Paseos del Prado, de Recoletos and de la Castellana, split the city on a north-to-south axis. West of Paseo de Recoletos, the Justicia and Chueca districts are a focus for fashion-setters and nightbirds; east, there's the smart Salamanca district, a 19thC residential and commercial extension. The office blocks, apartments and hotels of modern Madrid rise in glass, steel and concrete along the Paseo de la Castellana'a northern stretch.

Grand avenues, delightful plazas, narrow *calles* and shady parks are enlivened by people busily coping with a big city's routines and problems. Come evening, and late into the night, they are just as busy, strolling on their *paseos*, seeing and being seen. Vendors, clowns, musicians and artists add to the outdoor entertainment. For only a few months in winter, when bitter winds can sweep down from the nearby snow-capped mountains, does the weather dull the vitality of Madrid's appealing streetlife. In August many *Madrileños* head for cooler mountain areas and costas to escape the searing heat.

Visiting the Museo del Prado is almost obligatory. Its wealth of works by El Greco, Velázquez, Goya and other masters show Spain's great contribution to world art. There are also many Flemish and Italian masterpieces garnered by Spain's Hapsburg and Bourbon kings. Picasso's striking *Guernica* is in an annexe of the Prado, the extensive collection of Baron Thyssen will be displayed in another. Less famous is the Museo Nacional de Arqueologico which has many equally fascinating treasures from Spain's rich past. Quite a few more museums and galleries are well worth visiting.

The Casa de Campo is a big green space on Madrid's south-western edge with good facilities for sports, entertainment, exhibitions or just relaxing. Less than an hour away are the wooded Sierra de Guadarrama where resort villages cater to *Madrileños* recuperating from their excesses or eager to pursue active sports in summer or winter. As throughout Spain, *futbol* is the biggest spectator sport.

It is the urban ensemble as a whole in some areas of Madrid which is monumental, rather than many single buildings. But what the city may lack in this respect is made up for in full measure by the memorable sights in cities and places which can be easily visited on day trips from Madrid. In **EXCURSIONS**, the Collins Traveller introduces Segovia and La Granja, El Escorial and Valle de los Caidos as well as the extraordinary museum-city of Toledo. Organised tours are listed, why not try some of them? Whatever you do - have fun!

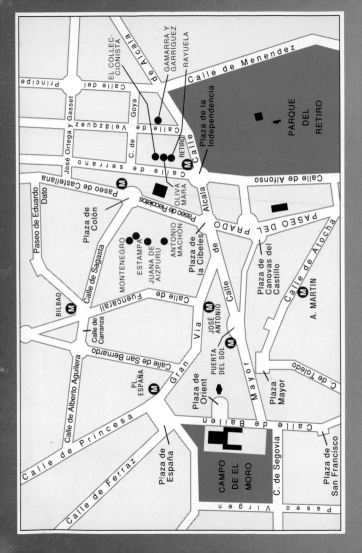

Art galleries run as businesses are good places to see what's currently being done in the fine arts. Madrid has many such galleries - most are in the streets on either side of Paseo de Recoletos. Here's a representative selection:

OLIVA MARA Claudio Coello 19.
M Retiro, Serrano.
Small gallery featuring lesser-known artists in 2-4 week shows.

RAYUELA Claudio Coello 19.
M Retiro, Serrano.
Often features painters and sculptors following the Cubist style..

EL COLECCIONISTA Claudio Coello 23.
M Retiro, Serrano.
Works of the famous Catalan, Tapies, can be seen and bought here.

GAMARRA Y GARRÍGUEZ Villanueva 21.
M Retiro, Serrano.
One of a number of good galleries in this and nearby streets.

JUANA DE AIZPURU Barquillo 44.
M Chueca, Colón.
Place to see work of new names like Barcelo and Xesús Vázquez.

MONTENEGRO Santa Teresa 7/Justiniano.
M Chueca, Colón.
A gallery which promotes little-known contemporary artists.

ANTONIO MACHÓN Conde de Xiguena 8.
M Chueca, Colón.
Works by modern artists. Also first-edition books and lithographs.

ESTAMPA Argensola 6.
M Chueca, Colón.
Modern Spanish artists. Solo shows or collections on a theme.

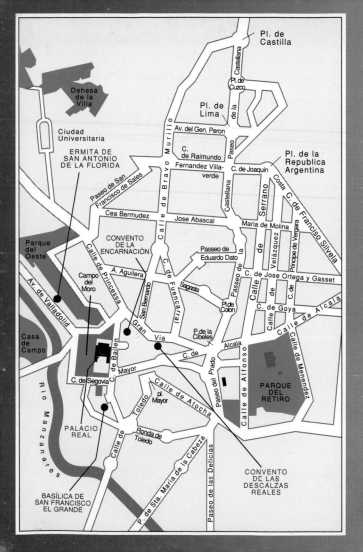

CONVENTO DE LAS DESCALZAS REALES

Plaza de las Descalzas 3.
• 1030 - 1245 Tues. - Sun., 1600 - 1715 Tues. - Thurs. Closed hols.
M Sol, Callao.
*Built in the 16thC and lavishly decorated, part is still used as a convent.
Tour of a collection of religious pieces, jewellery, paintings, tapestries.*

CONVENTO DE LA ENCARNACIÓN

Plaza de la Encarnación.
•1030 - 1330, 1600 - 1800 Mon. - Sat. Sun. and hols mornings only.
Covered by same ticket as Descalzas Reales.
M Ópera, Santo Domingo.
Spacious building (worth seeing) with rooms of unexceptional 17thC art.

ERMITA DE SAN ANTONIO DE LA FLORIDA

Glorieta de San Antonio de la Florida.
•1000 - 1300, 1600 - 1900. Closed Wed., and also Sun. afternoons
and hols.
M Moncloa, then walk through Parque del Oeste.
*Late 17thC hermitage better known as Goya Pantheon. His ceiling frescoes
show courtiers dallying with ladies of dubious respectability.*

BASÍLICA DE SAN FRANCISCO EL GRANDE

Plaza de San Francisco.
•1100 - 1300, 1600 - 1900 Tues. - Sat. Closed hols.
M Toledo, La Latina.
*Late 18thC with a neo-classical facade and 33-metre cupola. Six chapels
decorated by contemporary artists, including Goya.*

PALACIO REAL

Bailén (entry from Plaza de la Armería).
•1000 - 1245, 1530 - 1715 Mon. - Sat. Sun. and hols 1000 - 1330.
Closed (quite often) for state receptions. M Ópera.
*Huge Royal Palace built of local stone and completed in 1764. Now used
for state occasions. Guided tours of the richly decorated and furnished
apartments, and of Armoury, Library and Pharmacy and Carriage Museum.*

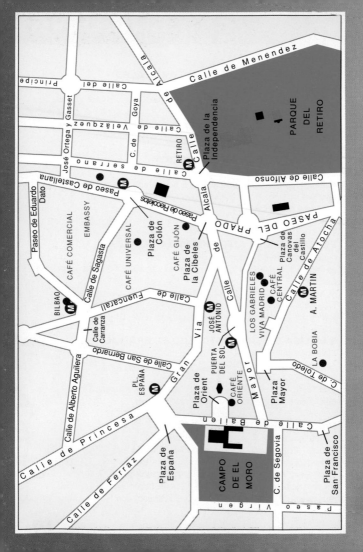

VIVA MADRID Manuel Fernández González 7.
M Sol, Sevilla.
Very attractive, authentic café. Busiest after 1800 with a varied clientele.

CAFÉ CENTRAL Plaza del Ángel 10.
M Sol.
Unchanging, old-style café. Lots of atmosphere, day and night. Live jazz.

LA BOBIA San Millán 3.
M La Latina.
1920s decor. Near El Rastro, and absolutely packed on Sundays.

CAFÉ ORIENTE Plaza de Oriente.
M Ópera.
A smart, pricey new arrival on the scene. Terrace with view across plaza.

CAFÉ COMERCIAL Glorieta de Bilbao.
M Bilbao.
Original café. Older regulars. Also popular with a younger crowd.

CAFÉ GIJÓN Paseo de Recoletos 19.
M Colón.
Traditional haunt of the literary set but the lively crowd is now mixed.

LOS GABRIELES Echegaray 17.
M Sevilla.
A recently restored bodega. Plenty of atmosphere from the surroundings and the people.

CAFÉ UNIVERSAL Fernando IV 13.
M Alonso Martínez, Chueca.
Post-modernist place for post-modernist people.

EMBASSY (Salón de Té) Paseo de la Castellana 12, Ayala 2, Padre Damián 42.
Elegant tea salon where the cakes and pastries are irresistible.

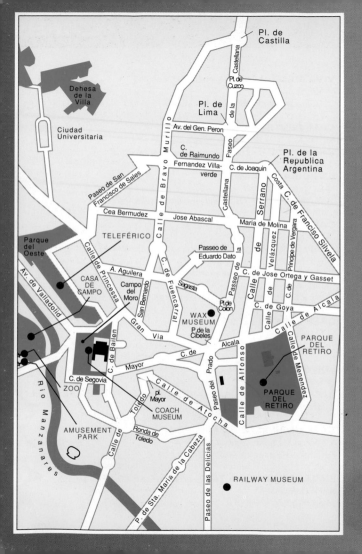

PARQUE DEL RETIRO
M Retiro.
Shady grass areas for romping, rowing on the small lake, horse and carriage rides, puppet shows, pavement performers, refreshment stalls.

TELEFÉRICO Paseo del Pintor Rosales.
M Argüelles. A short cable car ride.
Good views of the city and a means of access to the Casa de Campo.

CASA DE CAMPO
M Lago, Batán. Also by Teleférico.
Acres of grass and trees for picnics and games. Also lake with rowing boats.

ZOO Casa de Campo.
•1000 - sunset. M Batán. Also by Teleférico followed by short walk.
Favourites are the pandas (and the small tractor train). Animals and birds are grouped by continent in spacious areas.

AMUSEMENT PARK
Parque de Atracciones, Casa de Campo.
•1600 weekdays. Mid-morning on Sat., Sun., and holidays. Closed Mon. and weekdays Oct. to March. M Batán.
Teleférico followed by short walk. All the usual rides, fun and noise.

RAILWAY MUSEUM Estación de Delicias.
•1030-1330, 1630-1930 Tues. - Sat. 1030-1400 Sun. M Delicias.
Gleaming steam engines and other rolling stock. See EXCURSIONS .

WAX MUSEUM Museo de Cera, Paseo de Recoletos 41.
•1030 - 1330, 1600 - 2030. M Colón.
Good wax museum. Spain past and present. Also international personalities.

COACH MUSEUM Museo de Carruajes, Palacio Real.
•1000 - 1245, 1600 - 1745 Mon. - Sat. 1000 - 1300 Sun.,hols .
M Norte, Ópera.
A collection of fine carriages used by Spanish royalty.

OPERATORS AND TERMINALS

Julia Tours, Gran Vía 68. M Plaza de España. *Pullmantur*, Plaza de Oriente, 8. M Ópera. *Trapsatur*, San Bernardo 23. M Noviciado.
These offer similar tours and prices. Listed below are some of the tours these companies offer. Book with them or through hotels and travel agents. Itineraries can change. Men should wear a jacket and tie on night tours.

PANORAMIC
• Departs 1530, daily.
Drive along the main avenues and past the sights of Madrid. Highly recommended, good way of getting an impression of the city and its layout.

ARTISTIC MADRID
• Departs 0900, daily.
Visits to Palacio Real and Museo del Prado. (No visits to Prado on Mondays or to Palacio Real on days it is hosting state events).

BULLFIGHT AND PANORAMIC
• Afternoons, Sun. or Thurs. May to Oct. Advance booking essential.
Depart 2 hours before the bullfight for a drive through the city.

FLAMENCO
• Departs 2030 (to include dinner) or 2200 (show and drinks only). Not on Sun. Returns around 0130.
Drives along main avenues and past illuminated fountains followed by visit to a flamenco show.

SCALA MELÍA
• Departs 2030, daily. Returns around 0100.
Illuminations, followed by dinner and a show at Madrid's top cabaret venue.

SCALA AND FLAMENCO
• Departs 2200, daily. Returns around 0300.
Illuminations, then a show and drinks at a flamenco venue and at Scala Melía.

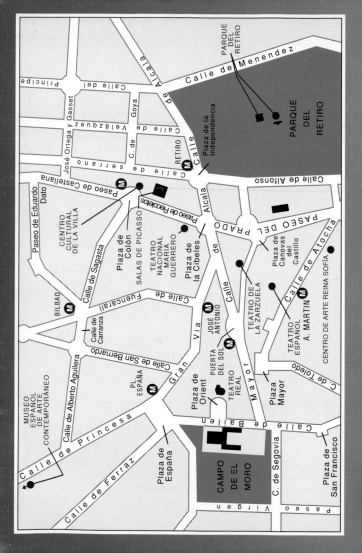

CENTRO CULTURAL DE LA VILLA
Plaza de Colón. M Colón.
A council-run venue for exhibitions, music, drama, poetry, children's shows.

CENTRO DE ARTE REINA SOFÍA
Santa Isabel 52 (opposite Atocha station). M Atocha, Antón Martín.
A converted 18thC hospital dedicated to all aspects of contemporary art.

PARQUE DEL RETIRO
M Retiro.
Palacio de Exposiciones, Palacio de Cristal. Exhibitions and performances.

SALAS DE PICASSO Biblioteca Nacional, Paseo de Recoletos 20.
M Colón.
Visiting exhibitions of modern paintings from the world's museums.

MUSEO ESPAÑOL DE ARTE CONTEMPORÁNEO
Av da Juan de Herrera 2. M Moncloa.
Visiting exhibitions, often better than the museum's permanent collection.

TEATRO REAL
Plaza Isabel II. M Ópera.
Until recently Madrid's main concert hall. The building, built in 1850, has now reverted to its original function as an opera house.

TEATRO DE LA ZARZUELA
Jovellanos 4. M Sevilla.
Seasons by Ballet Nacional Español and Ballet Clásico Español.

TEATRO ESPAÑOL
Príncipe 25/Plaza Santa Ana. M Sevilla, Sol, Antón Martín.
Site of a theatre since 1583, it presents mainly classical Spanish works.

TEATRO NACIONAL MARIA GUERRERO
Tamayo y Baus 4 M Colón, Chueca, Banco.
Home of the Centro Dramático Nacional presenting new and classic plays.

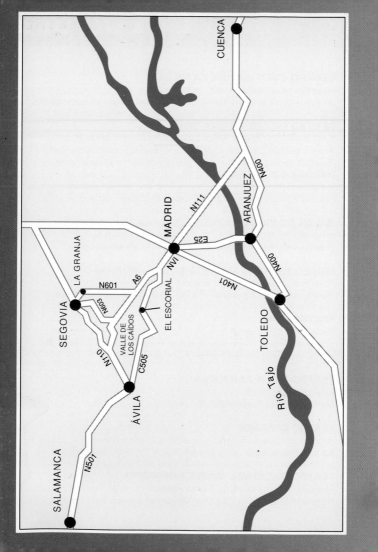

TOLEDO
• Full day Departs 0930, daily.
'A 'must'. See the cathedral, chapel of Santo Tomé, a synagogue, San Juan de los Reyes, Hospital de Tavera and a demonstration of damascene work.

ÁVILA, SEGOVIA, LA GRANJA
• Full day Departs 0830, daily.
Visits the city walls, cathedral and St Theresa's convent in Ávila; aqueduct, cathedral and alcázar of Segovia; grand palace and gardens of La Granja (on Mondays, those of Ríofrio). Lunch in Segovia. See **EXCURSION 3.**

ESCORIAL, VALLE DE LOS CAÍDOS
• Half Day. Departs 0830 or 1500/1530. Not Mon.
Visit Philip II's massive palace, monastery and royal pantheon and see also Franco's monument for the Civil War's dead. See **EXCURSION 4.**

ARANJUEZ
• Half Day. Departs 1500/1530.
Visits to the pretty town, grand palace and gardens.

SALAMANCA
• Full Day. Trapsatur only. Departs 0730. Tues. and Sat. May to Sept.
Visit the cathedrals, university, church, convent and Spain's most beautiful Plaza Mayor. Includes lunch.

CUENCA
• Full Day. Pullmantur only. Departs 0800. Thurs., April to Oct.; also Tues., June to October.
Tour of the rock landscapes known as the Enchanted City. In Cuenca visit the museums of Abstract Art and Archaeology, cathedral and main plaza.

STRAWBERRY TRAIN
• Full Day. M Delicias. Enquiries, bookings at RENFE and travel agents. Tren de la Fresa. Departs 1000 Sat., Sun., hols, May to October.
A steam train to Aranjuez. Girls in costumes serve strawberries and a brass band welcomes you. Visit the Royal Palace and gardens (see **Aranjuez***).*

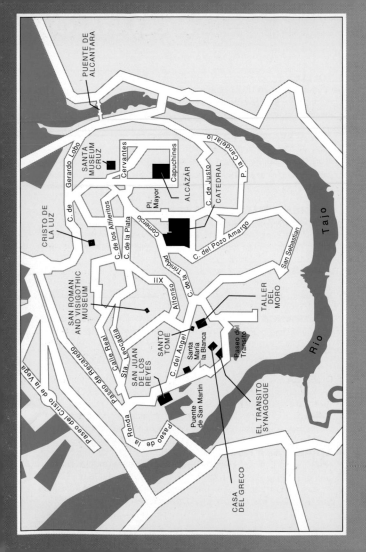

Toledo

70 km south west of Madrid by car N401. Trains from Atocha.

Spain's old capital with its rich and varied architectural assembly in tawny-coloured stone, is resonant with history, and filled with artistic treasures. Surrounded on three sides by the gorge of the River Tagus, it inhabits a very imposing site. No wonder this National Monument is one of Europe's top tourist attractions. No wonder too, that day-trippers, trying to see too much, leave exhausted, bewildered by all the beauty and 'all churched-out'.

At the end of the 2ndC, the Romans were building Toletum, on what had been a Celtiberian settlement. In the 6thC it became the capital from which the Visigoths ruled Spain. The Moors captured it in 712 and Alfonso VI, with the help of El Cid, took it from them in 1085, making Toledo the capital of Christian Castile. For a brief period, during the 16thC, it was the capital of newly united Spain. When Philip II gave Madrid that role, the medieval city finally entered the time capsule which today's visitor discovers; but Toledo is still the seat of the country's Roman Catholic Primate.

The Moors ushered in Toledo's golden period. The population grew to 200,000, cramped in a spreading huddle of buildings and cobbled alleys within the limited space on the defended outcrop. Moslem rulers allowed Jews and Christians to continue with their religions and cultures. Talents could flourish, economic prosperity ensued and Toledo became renowned as a centre of learning. Its scholars helped spread scientific knowledge and philosophy from Classical, Arab and Jewish cultures to Dark Age Europe. Prosperity, scholarship, and relative tolerance continued under the rule of Castile. Architecture and decorative work, notably *mudejar*, reflect the blending of influences. Ferdinand III and Alfonso X the Wise (1217-1284) encouraged the fusion of cultures. Not so the **Catholic Monarchs**, whose Inquisition persecuted Moslems and Jews and deprived Toledo of many of its most talented people.

In 1577, a painter from Crete, with an extraordinary talent, arrived to live in what was becoming a provincial town dreaming of its imperial past (see **El Greco**). The rich legacy of his paintings ranks high among Toledo's attractions. In many, he depicted his adopted town. How little it seems to have changed. Compare his *A View of Toledo* (El Greco

Museum) with today's view from across the Tagus on the south side (near the National Parador on Ctra Circunvalación). The Cathedral and Alcázar still dominate the skyline.

Then as now, the triangular Plaza del Zocodover (from the Arabic for market) was the heart of the town and it is a good place to start a walking tour. Building of the huge Cathedral began in the 13thC and took more than 200 years. Enter by the Puerta de Mollete, next to the main tower, and pass through the Cloister. Inside, the grand space and richness of Gothic, Renaissance and Baroque decoration are overwhelming. Beautiful stained glass, intricate wrought iron grilles, detailed sculpture in wood and stone, masterly frescoes and paintings.

Uniquely fanciful, the Transparente is a naturally lit, Baroque confection of painting and scupture. In the chapel below the dome, mass following the Visigothic ritual is still conducted daily. A silver and gilt monstrance weighing 180 kg is kept in the Tesoro. The Sala Capitular has a notable *mudejar* carved ceiling. Among a fine collection of paintings in the Sacristía are works by El Greco, Velázquez and Goya.

South west from here is the Judería (old Jewish Quarter) crowded with places of interest and fine examples of *mudejar* work. The Palacio de Fuensalida, a restored 15thC palace, adjoins the Taller del Moro where artisans employed on the cathedral worked, and where examples of their craft are shown. In a side chamber of Santo Tomé church is one of El Greco's best-known paintings, *Burial of the Count of Orgaz*. Casa del Greco is a reconstruction of a 16thC house and garden. Some notable paintings are displayed in the house and adjoining Museum. Samuel Levy, wealthy financier and adviser to the king, built the Sinagoga del Tránsito in the 1360s. The other remaining synagogue, small, white Santa María la Blanca (c 1200), is a masterpiece of *mudejar* work.

The Catholic Monarchs built the monastery of San Juan de los Reyes to celebrate a victory over the Portuguese in 1476. Its architecture typifies Isabeline Gothic. Chains of captives released in the conquest of Granada hang on the west wall. Note some amusing gargoyles. San Román, a 13thC church, houses the Visigothic Museum with a small display of art and artefacts from the period. Near the Puerta del Sol gatehouse is the small mosque of Cristo de la Luz (c.1000), one of Spain's best examples of early Moorish architecture.

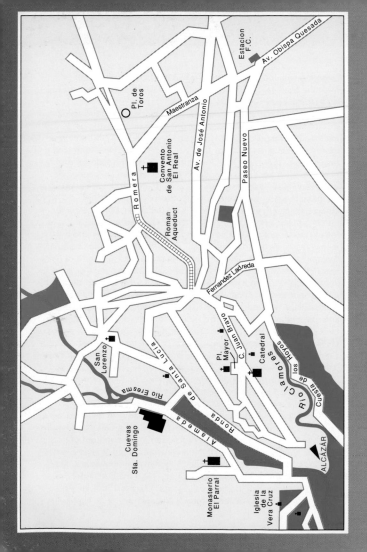

Segovia & La Granja

About 85 km north west of Madrid. NVI, A6, Exit 3 onto N603. Trains from Atocha, Chamartín.

•Church interiors: during services. Alcázar: 1000-1900. Cathedral: 1000-1900. Vera Cruz: 1000-1300, 1500-1900 Tues.-Sun. El Parral: 1000-1300 and 1500-1900.

Beyond the Guadarrama mountains, this beguiling small city is raised on a spur between two rivers. All turrets and domes, the fanciful Alcázar at its prow, it appears from afar like a ship aground on the Castilian plain. One of Spain's most important cities up to the 16thC, its stature then sank dramatically. The part of the city within the robust walls has retained much of its noble, medieval aspect. But time and the elements have taken their toll and there's a lot of restoration work going on. However it is still delightful to amble along narrow streets and to linger in evocative plazas like Conde de Cheste, San Martín or the café-lined Plaza Mayor.

Oldest of Segovia's three grand monuments is the Roman Aqueduct. Built in the 1stC, without mortar or cement, its two-tiered arcade of 118 arches runs for some 730 m with a high point of 29 m above the Plaza de Azoguejo. One of the finest existing anywhere, it is still used to bring water to Segovia (through a modern pipe laid at the top). The Alcázar was reshaped during the 1880s in a 'fairy tale' mould on the imposing site of a 12thC fortress which had grown in size and historical importance. Some of the original rooms remain and have been refurnished in the period of the Alcázar's greatness. The Cathedral is most famous for being the last major Gothic work done in Spain. Started in 1525, much of the work was done by the end of that century but it was not completed until the 18thC. Outside, it looks huge yet graceful. The tall, light interior is sparsely decorated. The city also has many interesting Romanesque churches and fine houses.

These churches, with their rounded apses and square belfries, were distinguished by covered porticos where artisans and traders gathered. Below the north walls the Iglesia de la Vera Cruz (True Cross, of which it once held a sliver) is a twelve-sided church built in the 13thC by an order of Knights whose secret rites were conducted in the two-storied rooms in the middle. The belltower is one of the best spots for getting a view of the city and Alcázar. Among a number of nearby

Iglesia de la Vera Cruz

Alcázar

Plaza San Martin

monasteries, El Parral, founded in 1459, is the most interesting and has a lovely setting.

Segovia is highly rated for its traditional Castilian cuisine, especially roast suckling pig - restaurant windows are full of them. The Mesón de Candido, Plaza Azoguejo 5, is considered a national institution. A modern National Parador (hotel), it is beautifully situated and is also a very good place to enjoy the local cooking.

LA GRANJA: 11 km south east (of Segovia), N601.
•Gardens: 1000-1900. Palace: 1000-1300, 1500-1800.
Fountain Play: mid Apr.-mid Nov. Thurs., Sat., Sun., hols at 1730.
Nostalgic for Versailles, Philip V commissioned Spanish and Italian architects and French landscape designers to create something similar, but smaller, in this high and wooded setting. French imperial style furnishing, mostly of Spanish origin, like the grand chandeliers from the local crystal works. Extensive, formal gardens and series of fountains, one of which spurts to about 40 m.

El Escorial

El Escorial

About 40 km. north west Madrid. NVI, C505Trains from Atocha or Charmartín stations.
• 1000-1300, 1600-1900.

The village of San Lorenzo del Escorial nestles in the foothills of the Sierra de Guadarrama. For *Madrileños*, it is a pleasant summer resort where they can escape the city's heat and many regard the austere, granite mass of El Escorial, which dominates the place, as the eighth wonder of the world. Philip II, for a time the world's most powerful monarch, commissioned Juan Bautista de Toledo, and then Juan de Herrera, to build this huge rectangle of monastery, church, royal pantheon and summer palace which was completed in 1584. Parts are still used as a college and a monastery.

The large Patio of the Kings is named after the six great Kings of Israel whose statues adorn the monumental domed church. All the monarchs from Charles V (with two exceptions) are entombed in the Pantheon. The Library has Spain's greatest collection of rare and beautiful books. In the Chapter Houses and New Museums, there's a collection of religious treasures and paintings by great masters. Charles III and IV decorated and furnished the Royal Palace to their Bourbon tastes. For many visitors, it is the simple rooms, where Philip II lived, ruled and died, which are the most memorable. Here he ruled all-powerful: then, latterly, pondered on all the disappointments of his weakening empire. From his austere quarters he could spy the elaborate proceedings of Mass and gain heart.

Guided tours start at the north entrance. Going in by the original main entrance to the west, it is possible to view parts of the building without being shepherded. Two lodges built for Charles IV, Casita del Príncipe and Casita del Arriba, can also be visited.

VALLE DE LOS CAÍDOS: 13 km north of El Escorial.
• 1000-1900. Closed some holidays.

The Valley of the Fallen (in the Civil War of summer 1936 to spring 1939). During the 1950s many of Franco's political prisoners laboured to tunnel a 245 m long basilica inside a granite outcrop and erect a giant cross (150 m by 46 m) on top in this lovely valley of the Guadarrama mountains. The dictator is buried in the basilica.

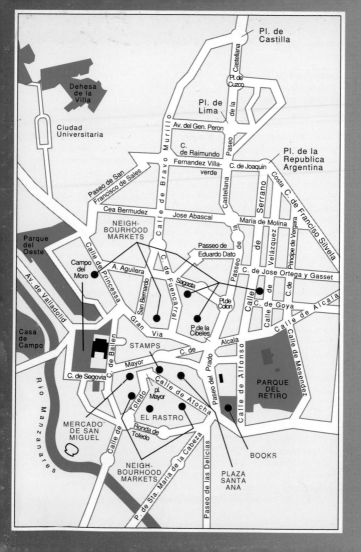

EL RASTRO
Plaza de Cascorro, Ribera de Curtidores.
•Best on Sun. 0900 to 1400.
M La Latina.
The full mayhem of one of Europe's best known fleamarkets breaks loose on Sunday mornings, to a lesser extent on Fridays and Saturdays. A myriad stalls rise in the warren of streets, raucous vendors wander around, and the world's for sale. Much is junk, rare finds are now few and far between. Bargaining is part of the fun in an experience not to be missed.

BOOKS Cuesta Claudio Moyano.
•Daily, but best on Sun. M Atocha.
Second-hand Spanish and foreign books. Among the pulp and ordinary hardbacks you might find some first editions, but the stallholder will usually be aware of their value.

STAMPS Plaza Mayor.
•Sun. and hols, 1000 - 1400. M Sol.
Good place to browse if your collection is weak on Spain and Latin America.

PLAZA SANTA ANA
•Sat. M Sol, Sevilla, Antón Martín.
Arts and crafts stalls.

MERCADO DE SAN MIGUEL Plaza de San Miguel.
•Weekdays. M Ópera, Sol.
All the sights and smells of a busy food market in an old, glass and iron building.

NEIGHBOURHOOD MARKETS
•Weekday mornings.
M Antón Martín, La Latina, Callao, Argüelles, Tribunal, Chueca, Serrano.
Free entertainment. Housewives and stallholders in a noisy exchange of banter. You'll find markets near these metro stations, ask for 'el mercado'.

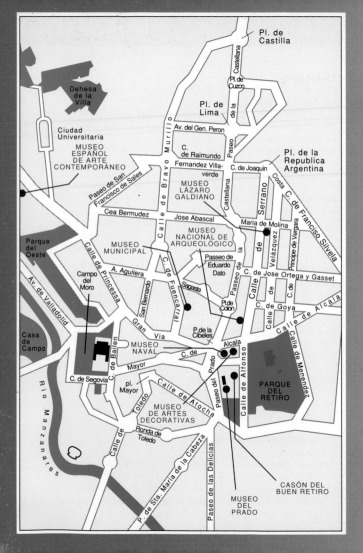

MUSEO DEL PRADO Paseo del Prado.
•1000-1700 Tues. - 1000-1330 Sat.,Sun. and hols. M Banco, Antón Martín, Atocha.
Immense treasure of Gothic, Renaissance, Mannerist and Baroque art. Neo-classical building. See **Museo del Prado.**

CASÓN DEL BUEN RETIRO Felipe IV.
•1000-1700 Tues. - Sat. 1000-1330 Sun. and hols .
Combined ticket with Prado. M Banco, Antón Martín, Atocha
Dramatic display of Picasso's awesome Guernica. The other half of the building is devoted to 19thC Spanish painting.

MUSEO NACIONAL ARQUEOLÓGICO Serrano 13.
•0930-1330 Tues. - Sun. M Colón.
Superb exhibits spanning pre-history, antiquity and Visigothic Spain.

MUSEO LÁZARO GALDIANO Serrano 122.
•1000-1400 Tues. - Sun. (closed August). M Nuñez de Balboa.
Fascinating collection of a wealthy Madridleño assembled in his mansion.

MUSEO MUNICIPAL Fuencarral 78.
•1000-1400, 1700-2100 Tues. - Sun. Closed hols. M Tribunal.
Exhibits tracing the city's development include a model of 18thC Madrid.

MUSEO ESPAÑOL DE ARTE CONTEMPORÁNEO
Avenida Juan de Herrera. •1000-1800 Tues. - Sun. M Moncloa.
A few Picasso and Miró works. Unexceptional permanent collection.

MUSEO DE ARTES DECORATIVAS Montalbán 12.
•1000-1700 Tues. - Fri. 1000-1400 Sat. and Sun. M Banco.
Popular Spanish design over the past five centuries.

MUSEO NAVAL Montalbán 2.
•1030-1300 Tues. - Sun. Closed Aug. M Banco.
Model ships include Columbus's Santa María. The Mapa Mundi of 1500 was the first Spanish map to include parts of America's coast.

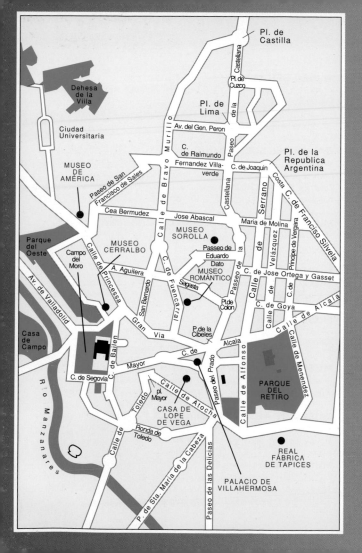

MUSEO DE AMÉRICA Reyes Católicos 6.
•1000-1400 Tues. - Sun. M Moncloa.
*For Europe, an outstanding collection of artefacts from the New World.
Special events are planned for the Columbus Quincentenary Celebrations.*

REAL FÁBRICA DE TAPICES Fuenterrabia 2.
•0930-1230 Mon. - Fri. Closed hols, Aug. M Menéndez Pelayo.
*Royal Tapestry Factory, the hand-making of tapestries based on Goya car-
toons and other designs can be observed. Works can be bought.*

MUSEO ROMÁNTICO San Mateo 13.
•1000-1800 Tues. - Sat. 1000-1400 Sun. Closed hols and 1 Aug. - 15
Sept. M Tribunal.
*Small palace and contents evoke aristocratic 19thC lifestyle. A few notable
paintings.*

MUSEO CERRALBO Ventura Rodríguez 17.
•1000-1400, 1600-1900 Tues. - Sat. 1000-1400 Sun. Closed hols and
Aug. M Plaza de España.
*Collection of tapestries, minor works by El Greco, Goya, other masters, and
some fine porcelain.*

CASA DE LOPE DE VEGA Cervantes 11.
•1000-1400 Tues., Thurs. Closed 15 July -15 Sept.. M Antón Martín.
Prolific writer's house and garden as they may have looked in the 17thC.

MUSEO SOROLLA General Martínez Campos 37.
•1000-1400 Tues. - Sun. Closed hols. M Rubén Dario
*Paintings of the Valencian artist, Joaquín Sorolla (1863-1923), displayed in
his home.*

PALACIO DE VILLAHERMOSA Paseo del Prado.
M Banco, Sevilla.
*Currently houses overflow from Prado. Negotiations are going on for this to
become temporary home (10 years) for the best paintings from Baron
Thyssen's collection, which would make this a major attraction.*

MUSEO DEL PRADO
One of the world's major art collections. Definitely not to be missed!
See MUSEUMS.

MUSEO NACIONAL ARQUEOLÓGICO
Iberian and Mediterranean culture through the ages.
See MUSEUMS.

PLAZA MAYOR
A grand, handsome square. To the south lies a warren of the old streets.
See PLAZAS, WALKS.

PLAZA SANTA ANA
A pretty square with many good eating places in the nearby streets.
See RESTAURANTS.

PASEO DE RECOLETOS
Take a stroll along this lively avenue and indulge in some people-watching. Great fun and it's free!
See TERRAZAS.

JUSTICIA/CHUECA
This is the lively, throbbing heart of trendsetting Madrid.
See NIGHTLIFE, RESTAURANTS, SHOPPING.

SALAMANCA
A smart residential area with many top shops and restaurants.
See SHOPPING, Areas.

PARQUE DEL RETIRO
A green retreat for relaxation, theatre and entertainment.
See PARKS.

TOLEDO
Make at least, a day trip to this historic, monumental city.
See EXCURSIONS 1.

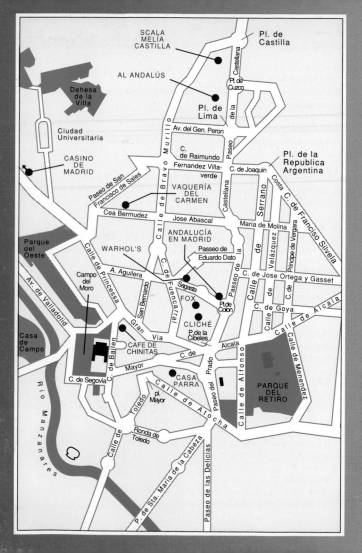

General

CASA PARRA Echegaray 16.
Steakhouse pub, popular with Madrid's foreign residents and near the best concentration of budget restaurants.

CLICHÉ Barquillo 29.
One of many high-style bars in this area, it's a 'must' on the scene.

FOX Hortaleza 118.
Long-time favourite of a fashionable crowd.

WARHOL'S Luchana 20.
Good music and, as the name suggests, pop art, New York decor.

VAQUERÍA DEL CARMEN Avenida de Filipinas 1.
A mixed crowd of all ages in this big, sumptuous place which looks like a 50s Hollywood set.

SCALA MELÍA CASTILLA Capitán Haya 43.
Presents the city's top Ziegfield-type show. With or without dinner.

CASINO DE MADRID Ctra. la Coruña. 28.0 km from city.
Bus from Plaza de España 6.
Huge casino with all the games, bars, three good restaurants and international cabaret.

CAFE DE CHINITAS Torija 17.
There's little to choose between the three top venues for flamenco shows. This one is central. Dinners (from around 2300) are so so. But going for dinner usually assures you the best seats. Shows around 2300.

ANDALUCÍA EN MADRID Plaza de Colón 2 (Torre de Jerez).
Dancing the sevillana is much in fashion. If you want to try, or just watch, this is one of the top new venues.

AL ANDALÚS Capitán Haya 19.
Another favourite place for swirling dancers.

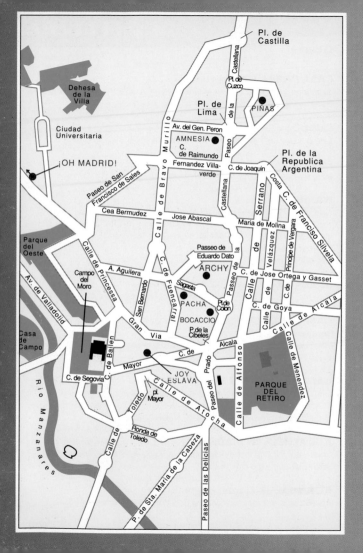

Discos

Essential feature of Madrid nightlife. Discos start swinging after mid-night. Inexpensive by international comparison. You'll have to pass the doorman's scrutiny. Places which are de moda one month may be pasado de moda the next. Here's a choice of some which withstand fickle fashion.

BOCACCIO Marqués de la Ensenada 16.
Over 17 years it's become a classic of the night for Spain's newsmakers of all ages.

JOY ESLAVA Arenal 11.
Every night, a costly fashion parade. This is where the beautiful people are. An air of money and success. Those who've got it. And those who crave it! Excellent lighting

PACHA Barceló 11.
Wed. - Sun. only.
An ambience similar to Joy's but a younger crowd.

PIÑAS Avenida Alberto Alcocer 33.
A small place with an older more mature crowd. A good bet in the modern part of the city.

¡OH MADRID! Ctra. de la Coruña 8.7 km.
carretera (road)
Best in summer.
Long summer nights in paradise! Gardens, terraces, swimming pool, good lighting, the latest sounds. And all the beautiful people too.

ARCHY Marqués do Riscal 11.
Very selective doormen. High-society venue with different ambiences in different rooms.

AMNESIA Paseo de la Castellana 93.
Don't go before about five in the morning. Stay to mix with people on their way to work. And try to remember not to forget where you are! Happily mad Madrid.

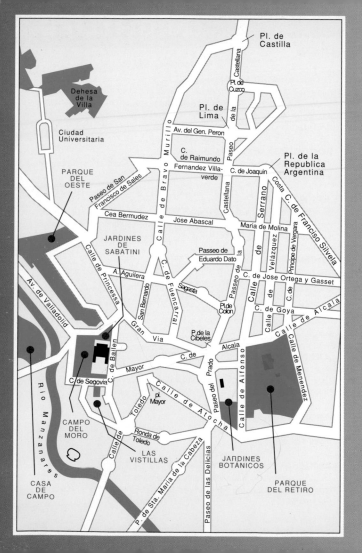

PARQUE DEL RETIRO

M Retiro, Príncipe de Vergara, Banco, Atocha.

350 acres of trees, lawns and formal gardens. A small lake for boating, a huge monument to Alfonso XII, numerous statues, two exhibition halls, an open-air theatre, refreshment stalls, horse and carriage rides, pavement artists, buskers, puppet performances. Liveliest in the warm months and at weekends, particularly Sundays.

JARDINES BOTÁNICOS entrance near the Prado.

• 1000-2000.

M Atocha.

Some 30,000 species from around the world.

JARDINES DE SABATINI

M Ópera.

A rectangle of formal gardens below the Palacio Real's north façade.

PARQUE DEL OESTE

M Plaza de España, Moncloa.

Long and narrow, it has the Templo de Debod (Egyptian temple) and La Rosaleda (rose garden) at the southern end. Popular with students.

CAMPO DEL MORO

M Norte, Ópera.

Walks, shrubbery and trees below western facade of Palacio Real.

LAS VISTILLAS

M La Latina.

Small garden area on higher ground with good views of city.

CASA DE CAMPO

M Lago, Batán. Also Teleférico from Parque del Oeste.

Madrid's lung, about 4,000 acres of trees, scrub grass and paths. Within its area there's a boating lake, sports centre, public swimming pools, amusement park, restaurants, the zoo, exhibition centres. Small buses connect the different sites.

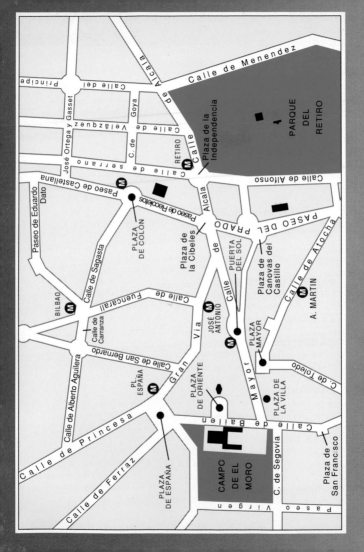

PLAZA MAYOR
M Sol.

Finished in 1619 during the reign of Felipe III, whose statue is in the centre, the large square was the scene of ceremony and pageant. Shops, bars, restaurants in the arcades, tables and chairs for refreshments in the sun.

PUERTA DEL SOL
M Sol.

Recent remodelling has tidied up 'the Gate of the Sun', vibrant hub of Madrid's, and Spain's, communications. Three metro lines, many bus routes, ten streets meet here and it's the point from which all the country's road distances are measured. There's a small statue of Madrid's emblem, the bear and berry tree.

PLAZA DE ESPAÑA
M Plaza de España.

A broad, open square dominated by the tall 1950s Torre de Madrid and Edificio de España. Features the monument to Cervantes and bronze statues of his creations, Don Quixote and Sancho Panza.

PLAZA DE LA VILLA
M Sol.

Finest of the old city's squares, it's surrounded by well-maintained 16thC buildings - Ayuntamiento, Casa de Cisneros and Torre de Lujanes.

PLAZA DE ORIENTE
M Ópera.

A pretty plaza, started by Napoleon's brother. Among many statues are some which were to have gone on the Palacio Real but were found to be too heavy.

PLAZA DE COLÓN
M Colón.

A 1970s development, surrounded by busy roads and tower blocks. Below is a car park, air coach terminal and the Centro Cultural de la Villa. Above, monuments to Columbus (Colón), the Discovery and the Constitution.

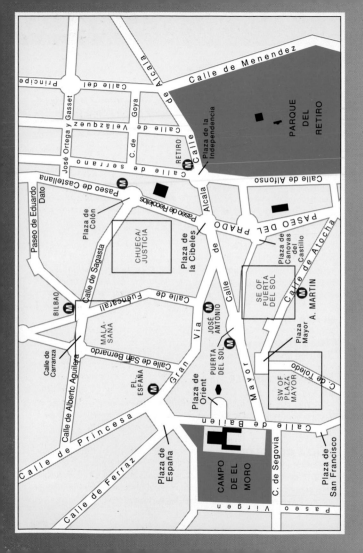

Areas

Four central areas in which to wander and find an eating place whose looks, menus and prices (displayed outside) appeal and we suggest a few places. Price groups: Budget, most main courses under 1,200 pesetas; Medium, under 2,000; Expensive, over 3,000.

SW OF PLAZA MAYOR M Sol, La Latina.
Traditional Castilian tascas and mesones, one after another in the medieval warren of Old Madrid. On Cava de San Miguel, Cuchilleros, Cava Baja, Puerta Cerrada and more calles and squares, follow the ritual of 'ir de mesones', stopping to sample the tapas before choosing one for the main meal. Cuevas de Luis Candelas, Cuchilleros 1, old, quaint, boisterous tourist haunt, good roast meats. Moderate. Esteban, Cava Baja 36, probably best on the calle. Moderate. Malacatín, Ruda 5, faithful clientele, simple, local cooking. Budget.

SE OF PUERTA DEL SOL M Sol, Sevilla, Antón Martín.
Madrid's best concentration of budget restaurants catering for discerning Madrileños. On Calles Echegaray, Ventura de la Vega, Manuel Fernández y González, Huertas and others in the area of Plaza Santa Ana, dozens of unpretentious, home-from-home restaurants offer good cooking from every part of Spain. D'a Queimada, Echegaray, excellent paella. Casa Ramón, Ventura de la Vega, Castilian favourites. On the same calle, both Jauregui and Bilbaino specialize in Basque cooking.

CHUECA/JUSTICIA M Chueca, Colón.
Feeding ground of Madrid's trendsetters where many new restaurants with adventurous young cooks have mushroomed. Gambón, Barbieri 1, small, meticulous cooking. Budget. Bar del Theatro, Prim 5, through a basic bar to charming bistro, Basque dishes. Moderate. Café Latino, Augusto Figueroa 47, an old style café dedicated to good food, serves until 0230 a.m. Moderate.

MALASAÑA M Bilbao, Tribunal.
No culinary highspots here but plenty of budget eating places, many with music. By day, a quiet neighbourhood; by night, a young, noisy atmosphere (and a bit threatening in the back streets).

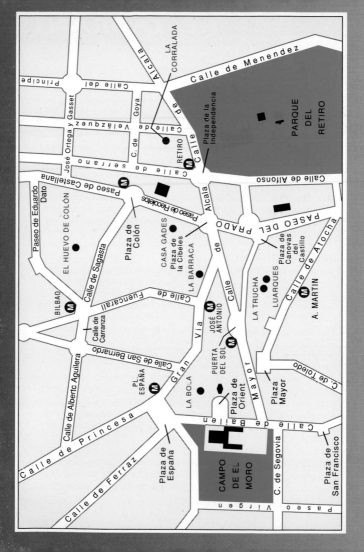

Budget

LA TRUCHA Manuel Fernández y González 3.
•Closed Sun. nights, Aug. •Budget. M Sevilla, Antón Martín.
Much praised for good fish specialities from the regions. Try 'pescaitos fritos de Málaga'. Arty crowd.

LA BARRACA Reina 29.
•Daily. MGran Vía. •Budget.
Beyond an obscure entrance, this intimate, old place specialises in paella and traditional rice dishes.

LUARQUES Ventura de la Vega 16.
•Closed Sun. nights, Mon., Aug. •Budget. M Sevilla, Antón Martín.
Closely packed tables, always busy. Asturian couple present regional favourites like fabada.

CASA GADES Conde de Xiguena 4.
•Daily. M Colón, Chueca. •Budget. No credit cards.
One of the owners is the dancer/choreographer Antonio Gades. Pizzas, pastas, steaks, salads at reasonable prices. And a fashionable crowd that comes to see and be seen.

EL HUEVO DE COLÓN Santa Engracia 15.
•Daily. M Alonso Martínez. •Budget.
Informal atmosphere. Great attention to preparing tortillas and other egg-based dishes.

LA CORRALADA Villanueva 21.
•Closed Sun., Aug. •Budget M Retiro.
Good, plain Spanish cooking. Always some politicians and journalists among a happy local crowd.

LA BOLA Bola 5.
•Closed Sun., Sat. nights in summer. •Budget. M Santo Domingo. No credit cards.
This place has all the ambience of a 19thC tavern. This is a good place to have cocido a la madrileña.

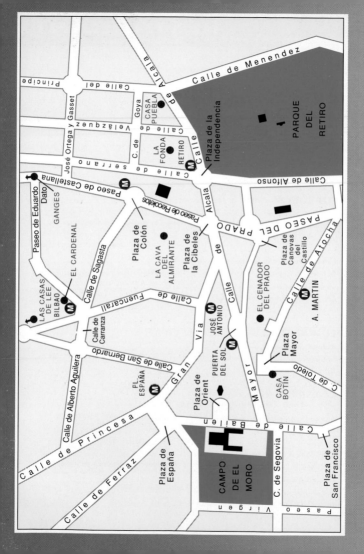

Budget/Medium

GANGES Avenida de Brasil 3.
•Daily. •Budget. M Lima.
Short menu of authentic North Indian dishes, including tandoori.

LAS CASAS DE LEE General Margallo 36 or San Felipe 4.
•Daily. •Budget. M Tetuán.
If you're in modern Madrid. These plain places serve authentic and internationalized Chinese food at very low prices.

CASA PUEBLA Príncipe de Vergara.
•Closed Sun., hols, Sat. in summer. •Budget. M Príncipe de Vergara.
Home cooking for a local clientele with big appetites. This is one of several similarly-named neighbourhood restaurants.

EL CARDENAL Cardenal Cisneros 6.
•Closed Sun., Aug. •Budget. M Bilbao.
Intimate and tasteful. Reasonably priced menu of high-quality cooking.

EL CENADOR DEL PRADO Calle Prado 4.
•Closed Sat. lunch, Sun. •Medium. M Antón Martín.
Spanish nouvelle cuisine. Elegant decor and attentive service.

CASA BOTÍN Cuchilleros 17.
•Closes on Christmas Eve only. •Medium. M Sol.
Roast suckling pork and lamb from an oven that's been going for 263 years. A big, bustling place, now catering mostly to tourists. Lots of atmosphere.

LA CAVA DEL ALMIRANTE Almirante 11
•Closed Mon. •Medium. M Banco, Chueca.
Kitsch decor, avant garde clientele, laid-back service. Interesting small dishes, good meats, sweets and selection of Penedes wines.

LA FONDA Lagasca 11.
•Closed Sun. •Medium. M Retiro.
Very pretty surroundings and efficient service. Catalan dishes and good selection of wines.

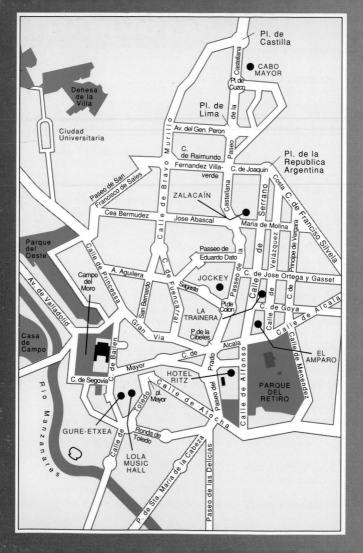

Medium/Expensive

GURE-ETXEA Plaza de la Paja 12.
•Closed Sun., Aug. •Medium. M Latina.
Basque cooking at its best. Traditional preparation of food. Unfussy, friendly.

LA TRAINERA Lagasca 60.
•Closed Sun., Aug. •Medium, no credit cards. M Serrano.
The best in seafood, a brightly-lit no fuss place. Very popular with tourists.

ZALACAÍN Alvarez Baena 4.
•Closed Sat. lunch, Sun., Easter Week, Aug. •Expensive.
•Allow for 10/12,000 Ptas per person (3 courses plus wine).
Superb food and service. Spain's top restaurant. It rates with the finest in the world and will beat most on price.

CABO MAYOR Juan Hurtado de Mendoza 13.
•Closed Sun., Easter, Christmas, 15 - 30 Aug. •Expensive. M Cuzco
Nautical decor. Justly acclaimed for imaginative seafoods dishes.

EL AMPARO Callejón de Puigcerdá 18 (off Jorge Juan).
•Closed Sat. lunch, Sun., Easter, Aug. •Expensive, M Serrano.
Distinctive nouvelle cuisine. Three smart, homely rooms in converted house. Careful attention to detail by discerning management.

HOTEL RITZ Plaza de la Lealtad 5.
•Daily. •Expensive. M Banco.
Young French chef presents inspired creations for memorable meals in a grand dining room overlooking garden.

JOCKEY Amador de los Ríos 6.
•Closed Sun., hols, Aug. •Expensive. M Colón.
Luxurious. A reputation for presenting the best in classic Spanish cuisine.

LOLA MUSIC HALL Costanilla de San Pedro 11.
•Nights only. Until 0400. •Expensive. M La Latina.
El Amparo's director and chef are involved in this cabaret venue where the dinner can be recommended. Pianist and singer follow variable show.

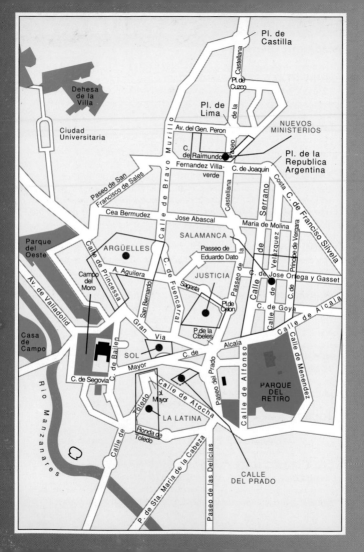

Areas

SALAMANCA M Retiro, Serrano, Velázquez, Goya.
A feeling of Knightsbridge or the Rue St Honore in this area - Madrid's most prestigious shopping district. Women, men and children's fashion, leather and accessories, jewellery, gifts, designer items, antiques. Concentrate on the parallels of Calles Serrano, Claudio Coello, Lagasca and Velázquez and the smaller streets which connect them, like Columela, Conde de Aranda, Jorge Juan, Goya, Ayala and Ortega y Gasset.

JUSTICIA M Chueca, Colón.
Chic fashion and design boutiques have blossomed along Calles Almirante, Conde de Xiguena, Argensola and half-a-dozen more streets in this compact area. They have the choice of creations from Spain's new, innovative designers.

ARGÜELLES M Argüelles, Ventura Rodríguez, Plaza de España.
Some good fashion and other shops along Calles Princesa (Multicentro at number 47), Martín de los Heros and Gaztambide.

NUEVOS MINISTERIOS M Nuevos Ministerios.
Variety of shops in Urbanización Azca. Also in nearby Calle Orense and Paseo de la Habana.

SOL M Sol, Gran Vía, Callao.
Big branches of the El Corte Inglés and Galerías Preciados department stores connected by pedestrian shopping street.

LA LATINA M La Latina.
From the metro, north to Calle Mayor and south to Ronda de Toledo, a maze of streets where small shops sell traditional wares.

CALLE DEL PRADO M Sol, Antón Martín.
Biggest concentration of high-quality antique shops.

PRÍNCIPE DE VERGARA M Núñez de Balboa.
Middle part of avenue has number of shops selling modern design household items and furniture.

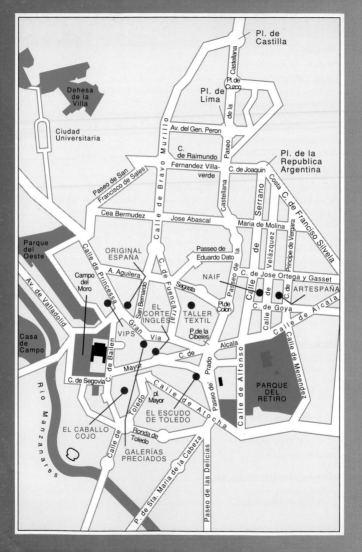

Gifts

EL CORTE INGLÉS
Preciados/Puerta del Sol; Princesa/Alberto Aguilera; Goya/Alcalá; Urbanización Azca
•0900 - 2000 Mon. - Sat.
Large, full-service department stores with an up-market image. Interpreters, money exchange, travel agency, delivery, shipping.

GALERÍAS PRECIADOS Plaza Callao; Arapiles/Glorieta de
Quevedo; Serrano; Goya.
•0900 - 2000 Mon. - Sat.
Also a large store group. Generally, a lower-priced selection. Similar services.

VIPS Princesa 5, Velázquez 78, Velázquez 136, Paseo de Habana 17,
Julián Romea 4.
Well-stocked drugstores which stay open late. Good fast foods too.

ARTESPAÑA Hermosilla 14, Ramón de la Cruz 22, Plaza de las
Cortes 3.
Government-sponsored chain of artesanías, features top quality items of traditional work from all over the country.

EL CABALLO COJO Costanilla de San Pedro 7.
Old and modern examples of popular handicrafts.

EL ESCUDO DE TOLEDO Plaza Cánovas del Castillo.
An artesanía with a full range. Emphasis on Toledo ware.

ORIGINAL ESPAÑA Maestro Guerrero.
Mainly ceramics with a big display of Lladró porcelain.

TALLER TEXTIL San Lorenzo 5.
Handmade textile and woollen goods.

NAIF Ayala 27.
A miscellany of items, some most unusual. Ideal gifts.

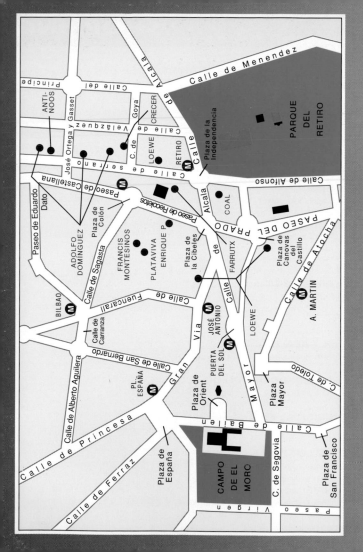

Clothes

ADOLFO DOMÍNGUEZ
Serrano 96, Áyala 24, Ortega y Gasset 4.
Creations for both sexes from the top international star of Spain's modern fashion flowering.

LOEWE Serrano 26, Gran Vía 8, Hotel Palace.
Sedate, elegant clothes for men and women. Also leather goods, shoes and perfumes.

ENRIQUE P Almirante 8.
Choice selection of good design. Other essential stops on this street are Jesús del Pozo (16), Ararat (10), Pedro Morago (20).

FRANCIS MONTESINOS
Argensola 8.
Imaginative clothes from this Valencian king of the catwalk.

COAL Valenzuela 9.
Creations for women from top designers like Antonio Miró, Manuel Piña and Antonio Alvarado.

ANTINOOS
Padilla 1 (corner of Serrano), Orense 12.
Shops for men. Latest fashions, classic clothes, shoes, accessories.

CRECER
Hermosilla 16.
Fashionable clothes and sportswear for kids.

FARRUTX
Serrano 7.
Very good choice of shoes at all prices.

PLATAVIVA Argensola 2.
Jewellery and accessories from most of Spain's top designers, like Ramón Oriol, Chelo Sastre, Joaquín Berao (own shop at Conde de Xiguena 13).

ESTADIO SANTIAGO BERNABEU Paseo de la Castellana.
• Sep. - May. M Lima.
Home of Real Madrid Fútbol Club. Accommodates 125,000 spectators.

ESTADIO VICENTE CALDERÓN Ribera del Manzanares.
M Pirámides.
Madrid Atlètico's ground accommodates 70,000 spectators.

FRONTÓN MADRID Doctor Cortezo 10.
• 1800 Mon. - Sat. M Tirso de Molina.
Betting on the winners is almost as exciting as this fast and tough ball game.

PALACIO DE LOS DEPORTES Avenida de Felipe II.
M Goya.
One of a number of multi-sports centres, this central venue often attracts the big basketball clashes.

HIPÓDROMO DE LA ZARZUELA Carretera de la Coruña.
• Closed in summer. See press for days, times, transport.
Horseracing and riding tournaments.

REAL CLUB DE LA PUERTA DE HIERRO
Avenida Miraflores, Ciudad Puerta de Hierro.
One of three exclusive clubs around the city. Two 18 hole courses. High green fees. Your own handicap card essential.

EL LAGO
Avenida de Valladolid (at Puente de los Franceses).
M Moncloa (then walk through Parque del Oeste).
Most easily accessible of city's good public swimming pools.

CASA DE CAMPO
M Lago, Batán.
Best place to head for if you want to get active. Tracks for jogging, swimming in Piscina El Lago, 15 all-weather tennis courts and, adjoining the Casa de Campo, nine holes at Golf de Somosaguas.

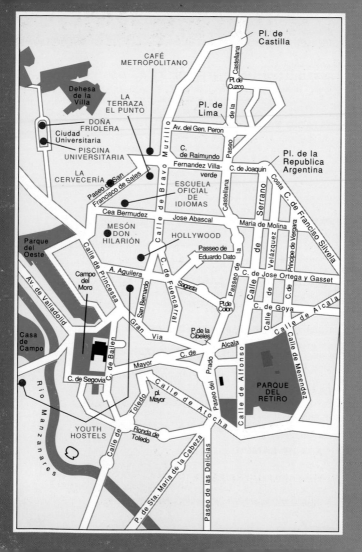

YOUTH HOSTELS Santa Cruz de Marcenado 28/ Casa de Campo.
M San Bernardo or Argüelles for the first and Lago for the second.
The first hostel has about 80 beds. More central, it's also more likely to be full. The second, the Richard Schirrmann hostel, has about 120 beds.

ESCUELA OFICIAL DE IDIOMAS Jesús Maestro.
M Río Rosas.
Spanish language and culture courses in all grades for foreigners.

CAFÉ METROPOLITANO Glorieta de Cuatro Caminos.
M Cuatro Caminos.
An old-style café popular with students throughout the day.

LA TERRAZA EL PUNTO Marqués de Lema.
M Cuatro Caminos.
A buzzing outdoor meeting point in the warmer months.

LA CERVECERÍA Paseo San Francisco de Sales 41.
M Moncloa, Cuatro Caminos.
A new cervecería where the beer is good and so is the company.

MESÓN DON HILARIÓN Hilarión Eslava 42.
M Moncloa.
For 'cervezas y tapas' and conversation. Quieter corners upstairs.

HOLLYWOOD Magallanes 1.
M Quevedo.
Inexpensive, fast food, music, friendly crowd, lively till very late.

DOÑA FRIOLERA Ciudad Universitaria.
M Moncloa.
Near the colleges, a disco bar where friendships start easily.

PISCINA UNIVERSITARIA Ciudad Universitaria.
Summer. Show your university or graduate card. M Moncloa.
No children. Relief from summer heat and easy meetings.

In the warmer months, outdoor bars open up all over the city. With about 40, the stretch along the Paseos Prado, Recoletos and Castellana has been nicknamed the Costa de Madrid - a fun focus of Madrid at leisure till the early hours. Different groups have their favourites, influenced by the type of music. Here's a pointer to some popular and fashionable places.

PASEO DEL PRADO Stress, young, Spanish pop. **NEPTUNO**, locals of the barrio, gentle melodies. **EL CHIRINGUITO**, yuppies, varied music. **EL INFANTE**, an upper-class lot, modern.

PASEO DE RECOLETOS Noisy street performers and vendors, strutting male prostitutes, couples and groups on constant paseos add to the interest of sitting at one of five terrazas. **GIJÓN,** an intellectual crowd, no music. **TEIDE**, mixed, small orchestra plays old hits. **RECOLETOS**, young and sporty, modern sounds.

PASEO DE LA CASTELLANA Nine terrazas between Plaza Colón and Glorieta Emilio Castelar are the haunts of the modern-living, young and beautiful. **REBECA's** post-modern crowd prefer ginger ale. At **CASTELLANA 21,** they go for Ballantines and imported music. **PASSPORT,** more mixed generation, disco music and a board of customers' photos (perhaps, the start of a modelling career). There are about a dozen more up to Plaza Castilla. **HISPANO**, near Plaza Doctor Marañon, attracts 25 to 45 year olds who like jazz. At **BAHÍA**, in front of the Bernabeu stadium, the music is pop and rock and the young hope to meet their soccer idols. Right at the top, **202's** customers come from the surrounding apartment blocks.

Other places: **PLAZA SANTA ANA** and surrounding pedestrian streets. **PLAZA DOS DE MAYO**, centre of Malasaña district. **CALLE JUAN BRAVO**, a string of terrazas, young and noisy. **PASEO DE LA HABANA,** fashionable artery off the Castellana. **PASEO PINTOR ROSALES**, bordering the Parque del Oeste, less trendy but ever popular. **LAS VISILLAS**, sunsets over the city. **HOTEL PLAZA**, top floor: mixed crowd, swimming pool and view over city.

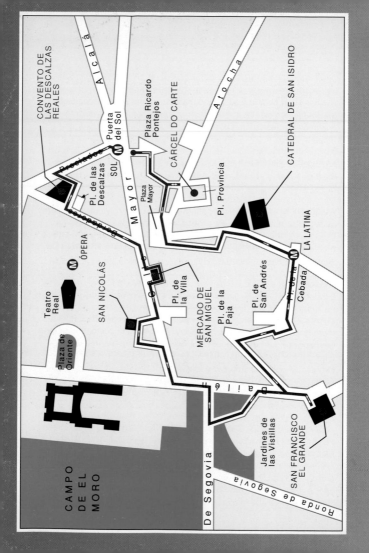

Calle Mayor

2 hr 30 min. M Sol.

On the south west, take c/ Correo to Pl Pontejos, lined with needlework shops. First right into c/ Marqués Viudo de Pontejos, more needlework and sewing-bits shops. Left into c/ Esparteros, small shops specializing in steel items. Facing the Pl Provincia, the Cárcel do Corte once detained wealthy wrongdoers and is now the Ministry of Foreign Affairs. Retrace your steps, then left into c/ Zaragoza, many silversmiths in this pedestrian area. Through the arch into the Pl Mayor. If the weather is good, you'll probably want to take a seat at one of the outdoor cafés to soak up the scene. [30 min]

Exit from the south-west corner into c/ Cuchilleros, lined with many *tascas* and *mesones*. You may be tempted into many more *tascas* on this walk. Left at Pl de Puerta Cerrada towards the undistinguished Baroque church of San Isidro, the city's provisional cathedral. On to Pl de la Cebada with its lively, old market. You may want to go left from here to investigate Pl de Cascorro, Ribera de Curtidores (scene of El Rastro), the maze of La Latina's streets and many intriguing shops. [20 min]

If not, go right to Pl de San Andrés which forms an harmonious ensemble with Pl de la Paja (see **Paja**). From the latter, left into tiny c/ Redondilla. Left again towards the big dome of San Francisco El Grande. Visit the basilica. As you leave, turn left into c/ de Bailén for a short distance, then left for a detour into the Jardines de las Vistillas, views across the city and, perhaps, a rest. [40 min]

Onto c/ de Bailén again, left to c/ Mayor. On the left is the unfinished Almudena cathedral, on the right a military headquarters. Go right along c/ Mayor then third left to see Madrid's oldest remaining church, San Nicolás, and its Mudejar tower. Back on c/ Mayor, cross over to the Pl de la Villa and its handsome civic buildings. Leaving, turn right to reach the bright and bustling Mercado de San Miguel. Left off c/ Mayor into c/ Bordadores, past San Ginés church, crossing c/ del Arenal, brings you to Pl de las Descalzas. Visit the convent. [40 min]

Exit left into c/ Misericordia, left into c/ del Maestro Victoria to the pedestrianized area around c/ Preciados and c/ del Carmen which includes two big department stores.

Finish at M Sol. [20 min]

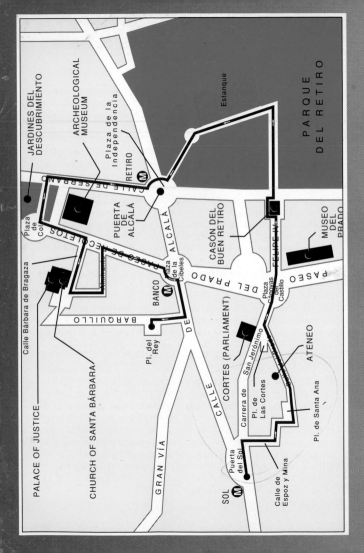

Retiro, Recoletos

2 hr 20 min. M Sol, Banco.

At the eastern end of the Puerto del Sol, turn right into c/ Espoz Mina, then left into tiny c/ Alvarez Gato which brings you into the delightful Pl de Santa Ana. The bars here and in surrounding *calles* may tempt you to go no further. Left into c/ del Prado, a street with many antique shops, passing the Ateneo, font of liberal thought. Continue to Pl de las Cortes where Spain's parliament meets in the rather unimpressive building across to the left. Right into Carrera San Jerónimo to the Pl Cánovas del Castillo on the Paseo del Prado. Cross over into c/ Felipe IV. On the left is the Hotel Ritz, on the right the Prado Museum and at the top the Cáson del Buen Retiro. Enter the Parque del Retiro through the formal gardens. [50 min]

As a minimum, walk along the *estanque*, a pleasure lake. Leave the park at the north-west corner to see the monumental Puerta de Alcalá. Cross over into c/ Serrano, the city's top shopping street. More good shopping streets to the right. The Archaeological Museum is on your left. Next come the Jardines del Descubrimiento with monuments to the Discovery and the Constitution. Walk through towards Pl de Colón. See what's on at the Cultural Centre below the square. [30 min]

Go left down the centre of tree-lined Paseo de Recoletos. For a small detour to get a taste of Madrid's trendiest area, go right into c/ Bárbara de Bragaza. Adjoining the Palace of Justice is the ex-convent church of Santa Bárbara (1750s) left into Conde de Xiguena and left into c/ Almirante. Lots of tempting boutiques, bars and eating places in these and surrounding streets. Right into Paseo de Recoletos again. If the terrazas are open, you can easily convince yourself you need a drink by now. [40 min]

Continue to Pl de Cibeles (see Cibeles), right into Alcalá, then right into c/ del Barquillo to the small Pl del Rey. It is overlooked by the Casa de las Siete Chimeneas (Seven Chimneys), a well-restored small palace from the 1550s. Return to c/ Alcalá and M Banco. [20 min]

Alternatively, you may want to continue up c/ Barquillo to discover more of the lively Justicia/Chueca district.

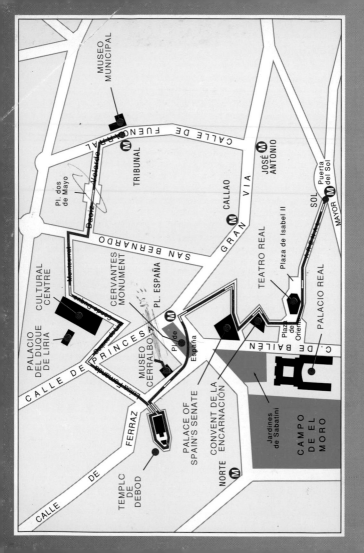

Sol to Tribunal

1 hr 40 min. M Sol, Tribunal.

Leave the Puerta del Sol on the west along c/ Arenal, which has some interesting shops, to reach Pl de Isabel II. Continue around the Teatro Real to Pl de Oriente. Across c/ Bailén is the monumental east facade of the huge Palacio Real. [15 min]

Leave Pl de Oriente on the north to Pl de la Encarnación with its convent. Left into c/ Encarnación, right into Pl Marina Española where the Palace of Spain's Senate is on your left. Continue into c/ Torija, then left into c/ Leganitos - both have the odd shop of interest - and you reach the Pl de España. [15 min]

After looking at the Cervantes monument, leave at the north-west end into c/ Ferraz. The Museo Cerralbo is on the next corner. Turn left at first pedestrian crossing to head for the Templo de Debod. After having a look at this ancient Egyptian temple and taking in the views from the elevated site, cross c/ Ferraz again to go right into c/ de Luisa Fernanda. Some good fashion shops in this area. Cross c/ Princesa, one of the city's main shopping avenues, turn right and have a look through the gates of the stately home of the Dukes of Liria. Right along c/ Duques de Liria, left into c/ Conde Duque to reach the entrance of the big, old barracks, now a busy Cultural Centre. See **What's on**. [45 min]

Right into c/ de Montserrat and you'll come across the impressive front and strange tower of an ex-convent and prison. Right into c/ San Bernardo, then left into c/ Daoiz to reach Pl Dos de Mayo, heart of the Malasaña district. Lots of bars and inexpensive eating places around here and terrazas in the warmer months. Best around lunchtime or early evening. [15 min]

Gran Via

Plaza Mayor

Accommodation: By comparison with other capital cities, Madrid offers accommodation at a very favourable price/quality ratio. *Hoteles* - H - are rated from one to five star. *Gran Lujo* is the top rating - Ritz and Villa Magna. An *Hotel Apartamento* - HA - offers full hotel services with accommodation in apartments. An *Hotel Residencia* -HR- does not have a full restaurant. *Hostals* -Hs - are much like hotels, usually with more modest facilities, and are rated one to three stars. But a good *hostal* can sometimes beat a similarly rated hotel. Tourist Apartments - AT - are rated from one to four keys, have self-catering facilities and usually require a minumum stay of one week. Guest Houses (*Casa de Huéspedes*) and Inns (*Fondas*) offer the most basic accommodation. There are a number of camping and caravan sites (rated Categories 1 to 3) outside the city.

The Tourist Offices at the Airport and Torre de Madrid offer assistance with finding accommodation. Spain's National Tourist Offices in your country will give information and provide names of companies in your country who deal with reservations in Spain.

For campers and caravanners, there's the central reservation service of the Federación Española de Empresarios de Campings, Gran Vía 88, 28013 Madrid. Telephone 242 31 68.

Airports: Barajas International Airport (*aeropuerto*) is only 11 miles east of the city, off the NII highway. It has a good Duty Free shop among the usual amenities. Porters are helpful and have fixed charges. Yellow buses run a regular service to a terminal below the Pl de Colón. Authorized taxis are relatively inexpensive (supplements are charged for the airport journey and for baggage). Avoid any other alleged 'taxis'.

Alcalá: This broad avenue runs north east from Puerta del Sol to Las Ventas bullring. Up to Plaza de Cibeles it is lined with the headquarters of many banks. On the Plaza de la Independencia is the Puerta de Alcalá, a granite, neo-classical gate completed by Sabatini in 1778 for Charles III.

Almudena, Catedral: On the site of a 9thC church. Its facade faces the Palacio Real's Plaza de la Armería. Started in 1883 as Madrid's

official cathedral, work stopped in 1940 and resumed a few years ago. The plan is a mix of Gothic and classical elements.

Aranjuez: On the fertile banks of the river Tagus, 47 km south of Madrid, this attractive, small town is popular with *Madrileños* and tourists for day trips. The Royal Palace was started by Philip II in 1560, but is more the creation of the 18th and 19thC Bourbons, and displays both Renaissance and Baroque styles. It's richly decorated and furnished. Most notable is the room covered with porcelain from the Buen Retiro factory. In the beautiful formal gardens, the Jardín del Príncipe, there's a small Rococo palace, the Casita del Labrador, built in 1803 for Charles IV. A small museum has a collection of royal launches. The buildings are open1000-1300 and 1600-1900.
Trains from Atocha. See **EXCURSIONS**.

Armeria, Museo: In the Palacio Real. Arms and armour, including the suits of Charles V and Philip II, swords of Cortés and Pizarro, and battle flags.

Arqueológico, Museo Nacional: Serrano 13. M Serrano.
Spain's most comprehensive archaeological collection from prehistory
to the Renaissance. Outside, there's a replica of the Altamira Caves
(Cantabria) which have some of the world's most outstanding rock
paintings. Other prehistory exhibits come from both Spain and the rest
of the Mediterranean area. The influence of early Mediterranean cultures is evidenced in the art of the Iberian people. From this period
comes the museum's greatest treasure, the imposing *Dama de Elche*, a
beautiful sculpture of the 4th - 3rdC BC. Also, the *Dama de Baza* and
the *Dama del Cerro de los Santos*. Most interesting from the Roman
period, is the collection of mosaics. The Guarrazar Treasure from
Toledo, an array of bejewelled goldwork, is the feature from the
Visigothic period. Moslem art (8th to 15thC) is represented by pottery,
metal work, stucco-work, carvings and some beautiful ivory caskets.
The continuing influence of their craftsmen can be seen in sculptures
and other exhibits from the Romanesque and Gothic periods. The
Renaissance ushered in the Italian influence, seen in the collection of
bronzes and furnishing, and in the Talavera ceramics, crystal from La
Granja and Buen Retiro porcelain. See **MUSEUMS.**

Ateneo: Founded in 1820 as a literary, artistic and scientific forum, it
was repeatedly oppressed by illiberal governments. Many illustrious figures have been members. See **CULTURE.**

Ávila: About 100 km north west of Madrid, Spain's highest provincial
capital sits on a spur above the Río Adaja with the Sierra de Gredos as
backdrop. The city has an outstanding example of unbroken medieval
walls, which have an average height of 10 m, surrounding the attractive
old town. There are nine gates and 88 towers along 2.5 km of ramparts
and a sentry path that can be followed. A fortified cathedral, and a
National Parador (Hotel), abut the walls. There are many churches and
convents associated with the reforming Carmelite mystic, Santa Teresa,
who was born here in 1515. Sugared egg yolks, *yemas de Santa Teresa*,
are the local delicacy to sample. Best view of town is from the Cuatro
Postes *mirador* on the road to Salamanca. Trains from Atocha,
Chamartín. See **EXCURSIONS.**

Dama de Elche

Avila walls

Ayuntamiento: Plaza de la Villa. M Sol. Also known as Casa de la Villa, the city hall was started in 1585, completed 110 years later and partly remodelled in the 18thC. The porter may permit entry to the principal chambers.

Babysitters: Not many hotels provide this service. Some may arrange for professional babysitters on request. Make enquiries in advance. You can also enquire locally about *guarderías* (creches).

Best buys/Souvenirs: Now one of the world's fashion capitals, Madrid has plenty to tempt the fashion conscious - clothes, leatherwear, shoes, accessories, jewellery. Children too have a great choice. Relatively inexpensive original artwork and prints of masterpieces are lasting mementoes. There are also good modern design houseware and decor items.

Craftwork from all over Spain is also available. Some ceramics, embroidery, fans and damascene jewellery are attractive and good value. Don't forget the excellent Spanish wines and brandies.

Bourbons: After the War of the Spanish Succession (1702-14) the grandson of France's Louis XIV was confirmed as Philip V, Spain's first Bourbon monarch. He was followed by Ferdinand VI (1746-59). Charles III (1759-88) became known as the *Alcalde* (Mayor) because of his interest in beautifying Madrid. The vacillating Charles IV (1788-1808) was led by his wife, María Luisa, and his minister, Manuel Godoy. Napoleon arrested Charles and his son, and placed his own elder brother, Joseph, on Spain's throne (see **Dos de Mayo**). Released in 1814, Ferdinand VII resumed the Bourbon line and reigned autocratically. One good thing he did was to create the Prado Museum. On his death in 1833, the right to the throne of his daughter Isabel II was disputed (see **Carlist Wars**). Alfonso XII (1874-85) reigned briefly, dying at the age of 28, and his wife María Cristina was regent for their son who became king Alfonso XIII in 1902. In 1923 Alfonso agreed to the taking of dictatorial powers by General Miguel Primo de Rivera. When municipal elections in 1931 showed a preference for supporters of republicanism, Alfonso abdicated. See **Juan Carlos**.

Bullfighting: Madrid's Plaza Monumental (Las Ventas) is the bull-fighting world's premier venue. Tickets for performances by the best *toreros* are hard to come by except from touts at hugely inflated prices. Probably the best idea for visitors who want to witness this essentially Spanish entertainment is to go with one of the tour operators. They provide a guide who gives an explanation of the performance and afterwards offers an assessment (see **CITY TOURS**). Children under 15 are not admitted. There are *corridas* (bullfights) daily during the St Isidro fiesta (May) and usually twice weekly during the season from April to September. Its aficionados regard the performance as an art form: a ritualized ballet in which the lurking danger to the man heightens the intensity. The fate of the *toro* is always the same.

Buses: Outside rush hours, the comprehensive bus network provides a good means of getting around the city - and seeing it en route. Air-conditioned, yellow micro-buses get you around more quickly and comfortably. Maps and *bonos* (saver tickets) from the EMT kiosk on Pl Cibeles. Some of the most useful routes pass through this plaza, like Line 1 on an east-to-west axis and Line 27 which goes north to south.

Car Hire: All the big international firms operate in Madrid, either directly or with Spanish associates. Smaller, local firms (whose leaflets may also be picked up at hotels and tourist offices) usually have lower rates. Look out for special deals and term discounts. Compare all-inclusive costs, as insurance and mileage charges often bump up the bill considerably. It's advisable to take out comprehensive insurance which must include a bail bond. By law you should present a valid International Driver's Licence but usually your normal licence will suffice. See **Motoring**.

Carlist Wars: Don Carlos, brother of Ferdinand VII, disputed his niece's right to the throne (see **Bourbons**) which led to the First and Second Carlist Wars (1833-39 and 1847-49) and much political upheaval. Isabel went into exile in 1868 and was replaced by a nominated monarch, Amadeo of Savoy, which displeased Don Carlos again, causing the Third Carlist War (1872-76). When Amadeo abdicated in

1873 the First Republic was declared, but it was shortlived and in the following year Isabel's son regained the throne.

Carruajes, Museo de: In the Campo del Moro gardens of the Palacio Real. A collection of carriages used by Spain's royalty and aristocracy.

Casa de Campo: See PARKS.

Casón del Buen Retiro: Built in the 17thC as the ballroom of the Hapsburgs' Buen Retiro palace, it's now an annexe of the Prado museum. One half is dedicated to 19thC Spanish paintings of the Historical, Realism and Impressionism trends, as well as the Catalan school, best represented by Rusiñol, Casas and Nonell. Picasso's *Guernica*, and his preliminary drawings for it, are displayed in the other half of the building. A huge canvas of powerful images in subdued tones, it was painted for the Republican stand at the Paris World Fair of 1937. In 1981, the centenary of Picasso's birth, the painting was returned to Spain from New York. See MUSEUMS.

Castellana, Paseo de la: This is the long, wide avenue that runs south to north, from the Plaza de Colón, past Nuevos Ministerios, Urbanización Azca and up into Modern Madrid. It is lined with old mansions (converted to banks and offices), modern commercial blocks, ministeries and hotels. See TERRAZAS.

Catholic Monarchs: Aragon and Castile were the two Christian kingdoms of Spain when Isabel and Ferdinand were married in 1469. She became Isabel I of Castile in 1474 and he inherited the crown of Aragon five years later as Ferdinand II. They married their daughter, Juana the Mad, to a son of the Hapsburg emperor. That marriage and the capture of the kingdom of Naples started Spain's European adventure. Isabel had set up the Inquisition and they gained the title of Catholic Monarchs from the Pope for their zeal in spreading the faith. Cardinal Cisneros was their staunch supporter and administrator. In 1492 they captured Granada, the last Moslem kingdom in the

peninsula, and expelled all Spain's Jews who would not be baptised. Also in that year Columbus reached the Americas.

Cera, Museo de: Wax figures from Spanish history as well as more contemporary Spanish and international personalities. See CHILDREN.

Cervantes: Miguel de Cervantes Saavedra, creator of the universal classic, *Don Quixote*, was born in Alcalá de Henares in 1547. He sought adventure and found it: wounded in the great naval battle of Lepanto of 1571; a few years later captured by the Turks and incarcerated in Algiers for five years. On his return to Spain, he began writing, with little recognition. In 1605, *Don Quixote* was published. It was widely acclaimed but yielded him few rewards. He made a meagre living from a range of other writing and worked on the second part of his masterpiece, finishing it in 1615. Still of modest means, he died in Madrid the following year on the same day as his great English contemporary, Shakespeare.

Children: They're made very welcome anywhere and at any time. See CHILDREN for some enjoyable distractions. Check the local press and enquire at the tourist office for information about special events.

Cibeles, Fuente y Plaza de la: M Banco. The goddess Cybele sits on a chariot drawn by lions. This beautiful fountain was designed by Charles III's architects as a grand feature for promenaders along the Paseo del Prado. Now she's marooned by the heavy traffic. On the south west of the plaza is the Banco de España (built 1884); south east, the white confection of the Palacio de Comunicaciones (1918), main Post Office; north east is the Palacio Linares, a ducal mansion; north west, another aristocratic residence, the Palacio Buenavisita is now occupied by the Ministry of Defence.

Cigarettes and Tobacco: Sold in an *estanco (tabacos)*. Many stock international brands. Spanish cigarettes are either *negro* (black tobacco) and strong like Ducados or *rubio* (blond) and mild like Fortuna. Cigars from the Canaries are relatively inexpensive. Pipe tobaccos are mostly strong and coarse.

Cinema: Spain has an active and adventurous film industry. Most foreign films are dubbed. Showings in original version with Spanish subtitles and advertised as 'v.o.'. There is a concentration of cinemas along Gran Vía and another along Fuencarral. First showing is usually at 1630, last at 2230. Alphaville, Martín de los Heros (Plaza de España end) is a four-screen complex which often shows films in their original language, as does Filmoteca, Torre de España. La Chopera (Parque de Retiro, open air on summer nights) shows popular films for a Spanish-speaking audience.

Cisneros, Casa de: This is the official residence of Madrid's mayor. Designed by a nephew of Cardinal Cisneros and built in the 1530s, its main facade on c/ de Sacramento is very richly decorated. A covered bridge connects it with the Ayuntamiento on the Plaza de la Villa. See PLAZAS.

Civil War: General Francisco Franco became leader of an army faction which, styling itself as 'Nationalist', rose against Spain's Popular

Front Republican government in July 1936. Madrid sided with the elected government and its people bravely resisted the 'Nationalist' siege of their city, and the accompanying heavy bombardment, until it finally fell on 28 March 1939.

Climate: July and August are blisteringly hot, June and September, almost equally so. During April-May and October-November, there is usually a pleasant combination of clear skies, low humidity and comfortable temperatures (15°-22° C). In December-February it gets chilly, and is often overcast, but there can be interludes of delightfully mild and bright weather.

Colón, Cristobal and Plaza de: Madrid was not yet Spain's capital when in 1492 Christopher Columbus (Cristobal Colón) first reached the Americas. Although the city can claim little connection with him, his discovery is proudly commemorated. At the top of a tall column his statue stands, facing west, and below the Jardines del Descubrimiento were laid out in the 1970s. Madrid, like all of Spain, plans great celebrations in 1992. See **PLAZAS**.

Complaints: Hotels, inns *etc*, restaurants and petrol stations have to keep a *hoja de reclamación* (complaints forms in triplicate). If your complaint is about price, you must first pay the bill before requesting the forms. One copy is retained by you, another is sent to the tourism department of the regional government. This is a valuable consumer protection measure which should not be abused by using it for petty complaints or grievances.

Conde Duque, Cuartel de: Large, austere barracks around three courtyards, designed by Pedro Ribera, built in the early 18thC and named after Philip IV's minister, the Conde Duque de Olivares. In an inspired and ambitious project, the city authorities have turned the previously run-down buildings into one of Madrid's principal venues for the performing arts and exhibitions. See CULTURE.

Conversion Charts:

TEMPERATURE

°C −30 −25 −20 −15 −10 −5 0 5 10 15 20 25 30 35 40 45

°F −20 −10 0 10 20 30 40 50 60 70 80 90 100 110

DISTANCE

kms 0 1 2 3 4 5 6 8 10 12 14 16

miles 0 ½ 1 1½ 2 3 4 5 6 7 8 9 10

WEIGHT

grams 0 100 200 300 400 500 600 700 800 900 1 kg

ounces 0 4 8 12 1 lb 20 24 28 2 lb

Cortes, Palacio de las: Carrera de San Jerónimo. M Sevilla. Spain's Parliament meets in this relatively small building completed in

1850. The large door in its neo-classical portico is used only for cere-
monial entrances. Two bronze lions beside the steps were cast from
cannon captured in one of Spain's Moroccan campaigns.

Courtesies: Try to remember that you are a guest in another
country and that the customs of your host are the norm here, not yours.
Two things you'll notice: Spaniards don't like being rushed; they don't
care much for forming an orderly line or queue. It's obviously impolite
to criticize their country, even if they themselves are doing so but they
will be pleased if you show an interest in them and their affairs. Two
important words: *por favor* (please) and *gracias* (thank you). Going into
a room, shop, elevator, or when formally meeting people, the greeting
is *buenos días* (good day) or *buenas tardes* (afternoon and evening).
Leaving, it's *adiós* or *buenas noches* (goodnight).

Customs:

Duty Paid Into:	Cigarettes *or*	Cigars *or*	Tobacco	Spirits	Wine
E.E.C.	300	75	400 g	1.5 *l*	5 *l*
U.K.	300	75	400 g	1.5 *l*	5 *l*

Debod, Templo de. Ferraz (Parque del Oeste) 1000-1300, 1700-
2000. 1000-1500 Sun. M Plaza de España. Situated on one of the city's
highest spots (Montaña del Príncipe Pío), is the small 4thC BC temple
donated by Egypt when the Aswan Dam was being built.

Dentists: See **Medical Treatment.**

Disabled: There is a new awareness of special needs, like toilets and

ramps, but generally facilities are limited. Be sure to make full enquiries of travel agents or holiday operators before booking and clearly state your specific needs.

Dos de Mayo: With the connivance of Manuel Godoy, (see **Bourbons**) Napoleon's armies had in 1807 entered Spain en route to fight the Portuguese, allies of Britain. With troops in place to support his demands, Napoleon summoned the Spanish royal family to Bayonne to enforce the abdication of both Charles and his son, Ferdinand. On 2 May (*dos de Mayo*) 1808, *Madrileños* staged a protest outside the Palacio Real to prevent the departure of the queen and her children. The French general, Murat, opened fire. Led by Pedro Velarde, the people took up arms. There was bloody fighting in Madrid's *calles* and *plazas* that day and night and severe reprisals by the French the next. So began the War of Independence in which the British general, Wellington, played a crucial role in assisting the Spanish. See **Goya.**

Drinks: Imported beers, *cerveza*, are available. *Una caña*, draught beer is usually lower priced. *Sangría* (of varying potency) comprises ice, soda water, red wine, brandy, fruit and juices. Sherry is called *Jerez* - *fino* pale dry, *amontillado* medium, *oloroso* heavier, sweeter. Spanish brandies, *coñac*, vary from the rough to fine (10 year or older *reservas*). There are many liqueurs and nearby Chinchón produces good anise ones. *Madroño*, made from strawberries, is a Madrid favourite.

Drugs: Possession of drugs is illegal and bringing drugs into the country is subject to very harsh penalties. Drug policies were more liberal in the early 80s but attitudes have hardened to try and prevent the use of drugs, and the associated crime, becoming a problem.

Eating Places: All of Spain's regional cuisines can be found in Madrid. The places to enjoy them range from simple *mesones* to the glittering elegance of top-rated restaurants, more than 4000 of them! Preparation is traditional or *cocina nueva* and much is now internationalized. Basque cooking, based on sauces, generally has the highest reputation. There are numerous foreign restaurants as well as franchise operations like McDonalds and Pizza Hut.
Meal times: breakfast until 1100; lunch 1400-1630; dinner after 2200. Grading of restaurants, from one to five forks, is based on the standards of facilities rather than the cooking. See **RESTAURANTS**.

Ejército, Museo del: Méndez Núñez 1. 1000-1700 Tues. - Sat. 1000-1500 Sun. and hols. M Banco, Retiro.
Military mementos of the Army Museum are displayed in what was once part of the Buen Retiro palace.

Electricity: 220 or 225 volts. Round-pin, two-point plugs. Wiring colour-coded to international standard.

El Greco: Born in Crete in 1541, Domenikos Theotokopulos had worked in Italy under Titian and Tintoretto before he arrived in Spain in 1577. He sought an appointment as a court painter but the king did not care too much for his work. Settling in Toledo, he made himself available for commissions, specializing in religious themes. Mannerism prevailed at the time and El Greco was to develop a unique, deeply spiritual style. His Italian apprenticeship and a strong Byzantine influence are always evident, the latter in elongation of form and perspective. He used vivid colours and often split his canvas into two compositions, an earthly scene spread below a heavenly vision. The portraits are done with darker colours and show reflective figures sure of their position in the order of the things. He died in 1614.

Embassies, Consulates: Tourist publications (*eg* the municipality's free city map) list Embassies, so do telephone directories. Hotel staff can also help you make contact with your embassy or consulate if required. *Eire*, Cladio Coello 73, 413 56 12; *United Kingdom*, Fernando el Santo 16, 422 02 08; *Canada*, Núñez de Balboa 35, 431 43 00; *United States of America*, Serrano 75, 273 36 00; *Australia*, Castellana 143, 279 85 04.

Emergencies: Dial **091** for the **Policia Nacional**. Concentrate on giving your location, nature of emergency and saying what other services may be required. **Ambulancias** - Cruz Roja 734 47 94; Municipal 252 32 64. **Bomberos** (Fire Brigade) 232 32 32. **Hospital** Anglo-Americano 233 31 00.

Escoria, El: See EXCURSIONS.

Escultura Al Aire Libre, Museo de: Paseo de la Castellana, below the overpass of Eduardo Dato/Juan Bravo. M Rubén Dario. Among the open-air displays of modern sculpture are Chillida's *Sirena Varada* and Miró's *Mere Ubu*.

Etnologia, Museo Nacional de: Alfonso VII 68. 1000-1400, 1600-1900 Tues. - Sat., 1000-1400 Sun. Closed on holidays. Artefacts from the outposts of Spain's former colonial empire.

Fiestas: *Semana Santa*, the holy week of Easter, is solemnly celebrated in even the smallest town. Toledo, Segovia and Cuenca have the more spectacular pageants and Cuenca also hosts an international festi-

val of religious music. The weeks either side of 15 May, feast day of
San Isidro, Madrid's patron saint, are given over to celebration when
different parts of the city or barrios compete in giving the best parties
and there's a big choice of cultural activities and sports events. The
procession of an ornate float, *la custodia*, through streets strewn with
herbs and flowers is the highlight of Toledo's grand and ancient rites at
Corpus Christi (late May-June). During the second week of October,
Ávila has religious and secular festivities commemorating Santa Teresa.
As hardly a week goes by without a fascinating fiesta in one of the
city's barrios or surrounding towns or villages, it's a good idea to ask
for details at a tourist office soon after your arrival.

Flamenco: Flamenco evolved after the establishment of the
Inquisition as the music of persecuted minorities who banded together
in the mountains of Andalucía gypsies of Indian stock, Moors and
Jews. Four separate talents are expressed in a full performance: *cante*
(singing), *baile* (dancing), *toque* (guitar playing) and *jaleo* (rhythmic
clapping and footwork). The best performers are said to have *duende*,
an inexplicable attribute. *Flamenco jondo*, profound and melancholy,

Su obsequio
pescados y mariscos
del pescador

Lleve los mejores
mariscos
para su casa

LOS PESCADOS
Y MARISCOS SON

expresses the deepest emotions. Lighter and livelier, *flamenco chico*, is more about sensuous love and sadnesses overcome. *Tablaos* at commercial venues usually present a mix of the two. See **NIGHTLIFE.**

Food : Castilian cooking is best known for its roast meat and game dishes. Here are a few suggestions of foods to try: *churros*, batter fritters for breakfast; *chorizo*, paprika-spiced sausage; *gazpacho andaluzía* chilled soup or 'liquid salad'; *sopa de ajo*, a soup of garlic, bread, paprika, ham and egg; *tortilla española*, potato omelette; *paella valenciana*, saffron rice, bits of meat, shellfish and vegetables, cooked to order (for lunch only); *menestra*, mixed fresh vegetables; *merluza a la vasca*, a casserole of hake; *bacalao a la vizcaina*, salt codfish with fresh tomatoes; *cocido madrildeño*, mixed stew of meats and vegetables (usually in gargantuan portions); *cochinillo lechal asado*, roast suckling pig; *perdiz estofado*, partridge casserole; *flan*, crème caramel; *queso manchego*, sheep's-milk cheese.

Goya, Francisco: He was born the son of an Aragonese artisan in 1746 and first gained his court patronage under Charles III, for whom he did most of his enchanting 'cartoons' as tapestry designs for the royal factory. His portraits of Charles IV and other royals are never flattering. There is much speculation that the Duchess of Alba was his lover and the model for the *Naked* and *Clothed Majas* paintings. Two masterpieces done six years after the events, *Episode of the 2nd May* and *Scenes of the 3rd May*, brilliantly broke new ground in artistic expression and vividly evoke the horror of the scenes of slaughter. The 'black paintings', originally done on the walls of his house, are the products of old age, deafness and disillusion. Yet, in his eighties he started doing work which could be classed with the later Impressionists. He died in Bordeaux in 1828.

Granja, San Ildefonso de la: See EXCURSION 2.

Gran Vía: The pulling down of old buildings to make what was to become Madrid's grand commercial avenue began in 1910. It runs from c/ Alcalá to Red de San Luis, then on through Plaza de Callao to the Plaza de España. At this end, the architecture of the hotels, the cinemas, the shops and the office blocks show an inspiration based on American design of the1920-30s, a touch of Broadway. However the street's grand days are now gone and smart Madrid is to be found elsewhere.

Guadarrama, Sierra de: These mountains (the highest is 2430 m) to the north of the city run on a north-west axis to link with the Sierra de Gredos. Together these chains are an important influence on Madrid's climate and are also conveniently close for a whole range of outdoor activities. Jagged, granite peaks, and slopes covered with pines and oaks, streams and lakes, small villages and leisure amenities attract *Madrileños* (many of whom have second homes here) to travel up for day or weekend trips. See **Wintersports.**

Guides: Tourist offices will provide lists of officially approved guides and interpreters for personal tours or for business meetings.

Hairdressers: Called *peluquería*. Many are unisex and prices vary greatly, so check before the stylist gets to work on your *pelo (hair)*. Three chains with good reputations, Llongueras, Gente and Macavi. Daniel Blanco, Juan Bravo 2, a smart salon offering beauty treatments.

Hapsburgs: Charles V (1516-56) inherited a united Spain with its Mediterranean and American colonies from the Catholic Monarchs, and the title of Holy Roman Emperor, with the huge Hapsburg domains of Germany, Austria, the Low Countries and parts of France, from his grandfather. His life was spent in resisting early revolts in Spain, fighting the French and combatting the Reformation. Before retiring to a monastery he gave up the German and Austrian part of the empire to his brother. His son, Philip II (1556-98), continued to waste Spain's wealth from the Americas on wars and fighting Protestantism. He was successful against the Turks at Lepanto (1571), took Portugal (1581) but his Armada against the English (1588) was a disaster and he finally gave the Low Countries to his daughter and her Austrian husband. During the reigns of the weak Philip III (1598-1621), and brighter but still ineffective Philip IV (1621-65) Spain's influence waned further. Yet it was a cultural Golden Age and artists like Velázquez and Murillo and writers like Lope de Vega, Tirso de Molina and Calderón bloomed.

Health: Too much alcohol and too many late nights take their toll. Pace your indulgence. Also your exposure to the summer sun. Choose

one of the bottled waters (*agua mineral*) and stick to it. Avoid eating ice, too many salads, mayonnaise and any place where standards of hygiene look deficient. If your digestion is feeling the strain, eat simple vegetable dishes, *tortillas*, chicken or plainly grilled fish. Health foods are available from *herboristerías* and if casual encounters are on your holiday menu, carry a condom. They are sold in *farmacías*, as are first-aid preparations and patent medicines.

History: See **Moors, Catholic Monarchs, Hapsburgs, Bourbons, Dos de Mayo, Carlist Wars, Civil War, Juan Carlos I.**

Hours: The *siesta*, Spain's traditional afternoon rest, is under threat in Madrid. Modern Spain cannot afford to sleep when its European competitors are working. Many businesses are now operating unbroken eight-hour shifts. Some government offices stick to the old times, others have changed. In summer, many places work one long shift, 0800-1500. So, it's all a bit confusing but here's a general indication: **Shops:** 0900-1330, 1630-2000 Mon.-Fri., 0930-1400 Sat. **Department Stores:** 1000-2000 Mon.-Sat. **Business Offices** 0900-1400, 1630-1900 Mon.-Fri. **Government Offices** 1100-1300 Mon.-Fri. (for business with the public). **Banks:** 0900-1400 Mon.-Fri., 0900-1300 Sat. See also **Eating Places**. Nightlife starts late - discos are busiest around three - and in some places goes on past dawn.

Juan Carlos I: The King of Spain was born in Rome on 5th January 1938, a grandson of Spain's last Bourbon monarch, Alfonso XIII. In 1962 he married Princess Sofía, daughter of the King of Greece. In 1969, Franco named Juan Carlos to be his successor as head of state and on Franco's death in 1975, he was proclaimed king. Don Juan Carlos set a course steering the country to democracy under a new Constitution (1978) which he has stoutly protected. With the queen and their children, Elena, Cristina and Felipe, he has created a popular and populist monarchy. The king is a keen sportsman and the queen is an enthusiastic supporter of the arts. They live at the modest Zarzuela Palace where there is little of the pomp and protocol surrounding Europe's other crowns. On his 18th birthday, in January 1986, Prince

Felipe took the title of Prince of Asturias and formally became heir apparent.

Language: Castilian Spanish is the official language. Young *Madrileños* are flocking to learn English.

Laundries: Hotels have laundry and dry cleaning services. A *lavandería* (laundry) or *tintorería* (dry cleaner) is likely to be cheaper. They usually charge by weight and need a minimum of 24 hours.

Lázaro Galdiano, Museo de: Serrano 122. M Núñez de Balboa. José Lázaro Galdiano, a rich financier and voracious collector, left his neo-classical mansion and its wonderfully varied artistic collection to the state, which in 1951 opened this fascinating museum of some 9000 exhibits. There would seem to be something of artistic value in almost every possible material, from every period. The building is full of surprises. Most outstanding are the collection of enamels, medieval work in precious metals, Italian Renaissance jewellery and the selection of paintings - Flemish and Dutch masters, Spanish masters (including El Greco, Velázquez and Goya) and some of the great English painters. See MUSEUMS.

Liria, Palacio de: Princesa 20. M Ventura Rodriquez. By written application on Saturday only. Closed August. Spanish speaking guide. The late 18thC Madrid home of the Dukes of Alba was destroyed in the Civil War and subsequently rebuilt. Fortunately, the rich art treasures had been taken into safekeeping by the Republican government. These include important works by Italian, Flemish and the greatest Spanish masters, especially Goya.

Lope de Vega: During a tempestuous life in Spain's Golden Age, Félix Lope de Vega (1562-1635) wrote some 1500 works comprising comedias, religious dramas, short plays, ballads and sonnets. The two other great dramatists of the period were also *Madrileños*: Tirso de Molina (1570-1648) who created the Don Juan character; and Pedro Calderón de la Barca (1600-1682).

Los Caídos, Valle de: See EXCURSION 3.

Lost Property: If you have lost something in the street, enquire at the nearest Junta Municipal (municipal office); in a taxi, at Alberto Aguilera 20; in a bus, at Alcántara 26; in the metro, at Cuatro Caminos station. In all events, tell the receptionist or a person in charge wherever you are staying. If the loss is serious, report it to the Police (c/ de los Madrazos) and get a copy of your statement. Promptly advise credit card companies, issuers of traveller's cheques and, if your passport is lost, your consulate.

Lujanes, Torre de: As almost the only medieval buildings remaining in Madrid, the house and tower have been much restored over the years. A Gothic doorway survives.

Mail: The main Post Office (*Correos*) is on Plaza de la Cibeles and is open for general business 0900-1330, 1700-1900 Mon.-Fri., 0900-1400 Sat. You may have your mail addressed here: Name, Lista de Correos, Pl de la Cibeles, Madrid, Spain. Collections (requiring your passport as identification) can be made 0900-2000 Mon.-Sat., 1000-1200 Sun. and hols. Stamps (*sellos*) can also be bought from your hotel or tobacconists (*tabacos*). Mail boxes are yellow and red.

Manzanares, Rio: 'You possess a fine bridge which is hoping for a river,' commented Lope de Vega about Madrid's small river. It has been cleaned up, directed into a wider, shallow channel and some leisure and sports amenities are provided along the banks. See **Puentes.**

Markets: For browsing or buying, free entertainment and local colour. See MARKETS.

Media: *El Pais* is the national daily newspaper with the highest international reputation. It gives wide coverage of Madrid's events and attractions. *Cambio 16* is the top weekly news magazine. *The Iberian Daily Sun* covers Spanish and international news. Leading foreign newspapers and magazines are widely available, most European ones

on their day of publication. There are both public and private radio stations, some providing constant pop music. Radio 80 broadcasts news in English 0700-0800 on 89 FM. Overseas services of some other countries can be picked up on medium wave at times or on short wave. TVE has two television channels. From June to September, Channel 2 features news in French, English and German between 1230 and 1300. See **What's On.**

Medical Treament: It is unwise to travel without a valid Travel Insurance Policy which provides substantial accident and medical cover. Take a copy of the policy with you and make a separate note of its details and any emergency telephone numbers. In Madrid, your hotel, or other places of accommodation, will assist in calling a doctor or making an appointment with doctors or dentists. Your consulate may provide lists of medical practitioners. You will be required to pay for each visit or consultation. Emergency cases are usually accepted at both public and private clinics or hospitals. Unless you have obtained a card entitling you to Spanish public health services, you will be charged for these services as in private clinics. On presentation of your insurance policy, practitioners and clinics may accept waiting for payment of large bills from the insurers. *Farmacias* (green cross sign) are chemist shops where prescriptions are issued. A notice on the door will give the address of the nearest 'on duty' chemist after normal hours. Prescription medicines are relatively inexpensive. Obtain and keep all your receipts for subsequent submission to your insurance company.

Metro: It's clean and will take you almost anywhere, but some connections are inconvenient. Get a plan of the network from any station. There is a cheap, flat fare and you can also buy 10-ride saver tickets.

Money: The peseta (ptas.) is Spain's monetary unit. Notes: 10000; 5000; 2000; 1000; 500; 200 and 100 (going out of circulation). Coins: 500: 200; 100; 50; 25; 10; 5; 1. Banks offer the best exchange rate but charge a minimum commission. Remember to present your passport for any transaction. The major international credit and charge cards are widely accepted, as are traveller's cheques in any west European currency or US dollars and Eurocheques supported by a card.

Montserrat: San Bernardo 79. M San Bernardo.
Begun in 1720, Pedro de Ribera's monumental design was never completed and at one time the building was a prison. Impressive facade and incongruous tower. See **WALK 3.**

Moors: The collective word describing Arab, Berber and other Moslems who invaded Spain from North Africa in 711 and rapidly gained control of the peninsula. Little is known about their period in Madrid. In 1083 their *alcázar* (fort) on the banks of the Manzanares was captured by Christian forces.

Motoring: If you want advice about driving in Madrid - don't attempt it! *Madrileños* drive very fast and very impatiently. Finding parking can be difficult. It is easier to use public transport, taxis, organized city tours and excursions.
If you are taking your own car to Spain get advice about procedures to follow in the event of an accident or breakdown. If these happen in a

hired car, contact the hire company for instructions. Parking prohibitions are usually clearly marked by painted kerbstones and signs. Some petrol stations close on Sundays and holidays so make sure you have a full tank before these days.

You need the following with you when driving in Spain: passport, current driving licence (international or EC), vehicle-registration document and bail bond (usually covered by car-hire agreement document), spare headlight, sidelight and rearlight bulbs, red warning triangle (if you're going on motorways). Minimum age for driving is 18.

Mudejar: A Moslem under Christian rule. Also, the architectural style incorporating Moorish elements, mainly 13th-16thC.

Municipal, Museo: Fuencarral 78. M Tribunal. The Municipal Museum and Library is maintained in what was the Hospicio de San Fernando, started in 1722. An elaborate Baroque doorway and plain facade was the work of Pedro de Ribera, as was the pretty fountain, 'La Fama', in the garden. A well-arranged and varied collection traces the city's development. Prize exhibits are a town plan of 1656 and a model of the city made in 1830. See **MUSEUMS.**

Music: There's music for almost every taste and Madrid attracts the world's top performers. Check in the local press, on billboards and at tourist offices for details. See **CAFES, CULTURE, NIGHTLIFE.**

Paja, Plaza de la: M La Latina. A harmonious architectural ensemble is formed by the Capilla del Obispo (16thC), the Plaza de San Andrés, the lantern-domed Iglesia de San Andrés (a 17thC reconstruction of a medieval church, now again being restored after Civil War damage) and the Capilla de San Isidro.

Palacio Real: Also called Palacio de Oriente. The site of a Moorish fortress, then the Alcázar, expanded by Charles V and Philip II, which was burnt down in 1734. Construction of its replacement was started four years later by Philip V who used the Italian architects, Juvara and Sachetti. Bernini designs for the Louvre in Paris were adapted for the facade. The square of the main building encloses a courtyard. Two projecting wings on the south side, the main front, form the porticoed Plaza de la Armería. On the west and north sides, huge basements take up the sloping ground, greatly increasing the impression of height. A decorated balustrade crowns the building. The interior is very sumptuous, mostly furnished in 'empire' style and much as would be expected of a flamboyant Bourbon monarchy. Today's royal family has more modest taste and does not live here. Tours are conducted in Spanish, English, French and German. See **BUILDINGS.**

Pardo, El: 1000-1300, 1600-1900 Tues.-Sat. and 1000-1300 Sun. and hols. Can also be closed on other days. A small Bourbon palace, in a wooded area 14 km north west of the city, where Franco lived during his dictatorship. More than 200 tapestries are among the lavish furnishings. The Casita del Príncipe, a small pavilion, and the Quinta, a ducal residence, can also be visited. Guided tours are availble.

Passports, Visas: Tourists holding a valid pasport of an EC country or of the United States and Canada do not require a visa to enter Spain. Those with Australian, New Zealand, South African, Japanese and some other passports have to obtain a visa from a Spanish consulate. Check with your travel agent, tour operator or Spanish consulate.

Pets: Get details about importation of pets from a Spanish consulate in your country and also check regulations about bringing the pets back home. Only a few hotels welcome pets.

Photography: Film, developing and printing is generally more expensive in Spain than in other countries. Rapid-processing shops give the standard quality service. Do not attempt to photograph policemen, military installations, any planes or runways. Photography, or use of flashlight, is not allowed in some museums and galleries.

Plaza Mayor: Building of this large, rectangular plaza (110 by 90 m) was started by Juan de Herrera for Philip II and completed by Gómez de Mora in 1619 when Philip III was king. Subsequently damaged by fire, it was much restored in 1853. Under a slate roof, there's a harmonious repetition of ground floor arcades, three levels of balconied windows, dormers and slim turrets. Residents would sell space at their windows to spectators of ceremonies (some gruesome) and festivities. The Casa de la Panadería (Bakery House), in the centre of the north side, had the rooms used by royalty. In the late 1960s, the plaza was pedestrianized, with a car park below. Various entertainments are presented in the plaza and it's the scene of the Christmas Fair. See **PLAZAS**.

Police: The *Policía Nacional* are the tough, smart-looking men and women in khaki and brown uniforms and berets who walk the streets in twos and patrol in white or tan vehicles. Report any crime to them and make a formal statement at their comisaría. *Policía Municipal* (blue

uniforms, white or blue cars) deal mainly with the city's traffic and enforcing municipal regulations. You'll see the *Guardia Civil* (green uniforms and tricorn hats) at immigration and customs posts and patrolling roads and rural areas.

Prado, Museo del: Spain's monarchs were great collectors and sponsors of art and this is the magnificent result. It was first assembled by Ferdinand VII in 1819 in the neo-classical building designed by Juan de Villanueva to be a natural history museum. Works from European parts of the Spanish realm, like Flanders, and by foreign artists whom some monarchs favoured, like Titian, other Italians, and Rubens, are well represented. Much of Charles I of England's collection was wisely, and cheaply, bought by Philip IV. The fine classical sculptures come from collections made in Rome during the 17th and 18thC by the Swedish Queen Christina and a Spanish ambassador. In the late 19thC, many pieces, including Romanesque frescoes, from churches and monasteries were added. There have also been acquisitions through donation and purchase.

The Prado is, of course, most acclaimed for the wealth of its works by Spanish painters, who include Yañez, Morales, Sánchez Coello, Ribera, Zurbarán, Murillo, Claudio Coello, Alonso Cano - and the greatest of all: El Greco, Velázquez and Goya.

Some remodelling, the installation of air conditioning and new lighting, as well as more modern methods of museum management, have improved the presentation, and preservation, of the exhibits. Serious students and experienced viewers of art will need no advice on how to go about getting the most from this big museum. For those with very limited time or who want to extract only the very essence of the place, the advice must be to concentrate on the three great Spanish masters. Just trying to take in their genius is enough for one day. The shop has a choice of guidebooks for all levels of interest (make sure to get one that's up to date) as well as cards, slides, posters and books on the artists. Sometimes, there'll be disappointment when it's found that one of the star paintings is away on loan. See **MUSEUMS, MUSTS.**

Prado, Paseo del: M Atocha, Banco. In 1775 Charles III commissioned this broad, tree-lined avenue to be the grand promenade of his day. It has remained so. Three fountains, Neptune, Apollo and Cybele are features. The paseo runs south to north from Plaza del Emperador Carlos V to Plaza de la Cibeles and is flanked by the Botanic Gardens, the Museo del Prado and other elegant buildings. Midway, the Plaza Cánovas del Castillo (and the Neptune fountain) is overlooked by the Hotel Plaza and the neo-classical Palacio de Villahermosa. To one side, the Hotel Ritz and the Bolsa (Stock Exchange) form a gracious semi-circle around the Plaza de la Lealtad, where an obelisk commemorates the loyal patriots of 2nd May 1808.

Public Holidays: Public Holidays are celebrated in Madrid on the following days: 1 Jan., 6 Jan., 19 March, 1 May, 15 May, 25 Jul., 15 Aug., 12 Oct., 1 Nov., 9 Nov., 8 Dec., 25 Dec. and on the variable feast days of Good Friday, Easter Monday and Corpus Christi.

Public Toilets: There are few. The best idea is to choose a bar or café, use its facilities, then have something to drink there.

Puentes: Puente de Segovia. M Ópera or La Latina, then a walk west. Puente de Toledo, M Pirámides.The Puente de Segovia, opened in 1584, is the oldest remaining bridge over the Manzanares. It's plain, solid and severe, showing the touch of its architect, Juan de Herrera, who was commissioned by Philip II. About 150 years later, Pedro de Ribera, working for Philip V, built the much more elaborate Puente de Toledo, with its buttresses, balconies and two small chapels half way along. The contrasting styles demonstrate the difference in tastes between an early Hapsburg and the first Bourbon monarch.

Railways: Madrid is the hub of Spain's railway network. Chamartín station serves the north, the east and France. Atocha is the terminus for services to the south, the west and Portugal. Norte, or Príncipe Pío, links with the north west. As there are different types of mainline trains and fare structures, it is wise to consult a travel agent or RENFE central office for information.

Recoletos, Paseo de: M Banco, Colón. Runs from the Plaza de Cibeles to Plaza de Colón, linking with the Paseo del Prado and Paseo de la Castellana to complete the city's main avenue on a north-south axis. It is lined with terrace blocks, the mansion of the Marqués de Salamanca (now the Mortgage Bank) and the National Library and is probably the most favoured stretch for *Madrileños* to take a *paseo*.

Religious Services: Your consulate will be able to provide information on places of worship and times of services. Among Catholic churches serving the foreign community are: British: Núñez de Balboa 43; French: Lagasca 87; Italian: Travesca del iombo 1; North American: Avda Alfonso XIII 165; Polish Donos Cortés 63. Other churches and centres include: Church of England: Hermosilla 45; Protestant Inter-Denominational Padre: Damián 23; Seventh Day Adventist: Alenza 6; Latter Day Saints: Paseo de la Habana 202; Jewish Community: Balmes 3; Islamic Centre Alonso Cano 3.

Riofrío: Palace: 1000-1300, 1600-1900. 10 km south west of Segovia. 18thC palace of Italian design, surrounded by oak woods and

a deer park. Hunting gear and stuffed animals in a Hunting Museum.

San Isidro, Catedral de: Toledo 49. M La Latina. Built in the 1620s by Jesuits in the Baroque style. Subsequently altered and dedicated to Madrid's patron saint. It serves as the city's temporary cathedral. The adjoining college has an attractive cloister. See **WALK 1.**

Segovia: See **EXCURSIONS.** Also **Puentes.**

Sereno: In times past *serenos* held the keys of neighbourhood blocks and let people in at night. Now, more youthful and robust, they patrol the streets armed with truncheon, torch and an alarm.

Sports: See **SPORTS.** Local tourist offices can provide more information, including addresses of sports federations. Hoardings and newspapers advertise major spectator events.

Tapas and Tascas: *Tascas* are bars which you go to as much for a drink, like a *caña* (draught beer), as something to eat. Many serve

excellent *tapas* - appetizers, ranging from olives, nuts or crisps to small and tasty portions of meats, seafoods, omelettes, salads or vegetables. All are temptingly displayed on the counter so you can indicate what you want. Some are served hot. *Raciones* are larger portions.

Taurino, Museo: Plaza Monumental de Las Ventas, Patio de Caballos, Alcalá. Tues.-Sun. 0900-1500. M Ventas.
Attached to the country's busiest bullring, this museum shows all the trappings of the *corrida de toros* and some famous *toreros*.

Taxis: They are plentiful and inexpensive by international comparison. Either black or white with a red stripe, they stand at ranks or can be hailed. They're free when showing a *libre* sign on the windscreen and a small green light on the roof. A list of supplements which may be added to the metered fare is shown in the cab.

Telephone, Telex, Fax: Hotels tend to add a big margin to the cost of communications services.

Telephone: Cheap rate is from 2200-0800. Coin-operated booths require 5, 25 or 100 peseta coins. Place coins in sloping groove at top of coin box. Lift receiver, check for dial tone, then dial. Coins will drop into box as needed. Codes for Spanish provinces and other countries are given in the booths. For local calls dial the number only. For international calls, after the tone, dial 07, wait for second tone, then dial country code plus area code (exclude initial plus number. The Operator is available on 008. At the Telefónica office, Gran Vía 28, payment is made at a desk after the call and assistance is available if required (0900-1300, 1700-1900 Mon.-Sat., 1000-1400, 1700-2100 Sun. *Telex and Fax* at main Post Office (Pl de la Cibeles) and from business services bureaux. *Telegram*: by telephone on 222 20 00 and at Post Offices (24 hrs at Pl de la Cibeles).

Tertulia: A meeting in some public place where regulars get together to talk and set the world to rights, from their particular viewpoint. A fading custom, it still happens in places like the Café Gijón and the bar of the Hotel Velázquez.

Time Differences: Same time zone as Western Europe: one hour ahead of GMT and 6-12 hours later than the USA.

Tipping: Although it may not be shown separately, a service charge is included on all hotel and restaurant bills. It's still the practice to leave around 5% to 10% in restaurants and to tip hotel staff for special services. At the bar, leave a token tip; 5 to 10% for table service. Taxi drivers, hairdressers and tour guides get around 10%. Lavatory attendants, doormen, shoeshines, car-parking attendants: 25, 50 or 100 ptas.

Toledo: See EXCURSIONS, **Puentes.**

Tuna: Not the fish, but students, dressed in the style of Spain's Golden Age, and forming a band of troubadours which moves around the bars and restaurants in hope of generous audiences.

Universitaria, Ciudad: M Moncloa. Development of this sprawling

site started in 1927 under the Primo de Rivera dictatorship. Many buildings were destroyed in the Civil War during the siege of Madrid. Their replacements display the dullness of the Franco period and modern additions to the campus are functional but uninspired. Spain's biggest university was founded in Alcalá de Henares by Cardinal Cisneros in 1498. When it moved to Madrid it was first located in the area north of Gran Vía.

Velázquez, Diego: Velázquez began studying art as a teenager in Seville where he was born in 1599. Aged 24, he moved to Madrid and became Court painter to Philip IV, a position he held until his death in 1660. His output on religious subjects was small and largely limited to his early years. Naturalism was his forte and his paintings are free from strident symbolism or propaganda for the subjects. He painted members of the royalty family, people at Court (including many dwarfs), mythological and historical scenes. His particular triumph was over aerial perspective and he was exceptionally successful in pulling the viewer into the picture, something he perfected in what is probably his most famous work, *Las Meninas*. Also in the Prado are his *Los Borrachos* (Drunkards), *Las Hilanderas* (Spinners) and *Las Lanzas* (Lances).

Villa: The old Castilian term for a small fortified town. Spain's capital rather oddly clings to being a *villa* rather than assuming a much grander title.

What's On: Look for leaflets and posters at your hotel, tourist offices, cultural venues. Advertisements of events are posted around the city. *Guia del Ocio* is a weekly listings publication. *El Pais*, the national daily, has good listings, previews and reviews. See **Media.**

Wine: *Vino* is *tinto* (red), *blanco* (white) or *rosado* (rosé). Spain produces some excellent wines in its *denominaciones de origen*, officially demarcated and controlled wine-producing regions, of which Rioja is the best known internationally, especially for its full-bodied, oaky reds. Many restaurants will have a *vino de la casa*, house wine, from La Mancha or Valdepe as the regions nearest Madrid. Regional restaurants will feature their region's wines, like Ribeiro from Galicia and Penedes from Cataluña. *Vinos de terreno* are simple, inexpensive wines from local bodegas, always best drunk young, which lubricate most fiestas. Before ordering a wine, see what local people are drinking or ask the waiter for advice. If wines are a special interest, invest in a good one.

Wintersports: Madrid has the good fortune of being able to offer the winter combination of a capital city's comfort, sophistication and entertainment with good wintersports facilities less than two hours away in the Sierra de Guadarrama at Puerto de Navacerrada, Valcotos and Valdesquí. There are runs of all grades of difficulty, T-bar and chair lifts, Spanish Ski School classes. Accommodation and other amenities are being extended. You may see the King on the slopes!

QC 98